Everyman

To order additional copies, please contact us.
BookSurge, LLC
www.booksurge.com
1-866-308-6235
orders@booksurge.com

Everyman

(Foot "Prince" in the snow tales of an African American Transit General Manager)

James Whitfield Ellison
Robert H. Prince JR.

2006

Everyman

ACKNOWLEDGEMENTS

To my family, my wife Judith who, without her support, encouragement and love, this journey would not have been possible. I thank you for our children and your ability to be a wife, mom, and educator to so many. You make me so proud. To Lenny Coley I truly miss him and have so much to be thankful to him for, his daughter, his willingness to always help, his passion for the T and my introduction into his world of Transit. To my children Roberta and Anthony you are my heart and I am so proud to be your dad. To my grandchildren Zachary and Jessica you are the future, and I have great faith in you. To my Father Robert Prince Sr., thanks for being my dad, my mentor, my friend. My mother Mary Prince, I thank you for compassion in seeing people for the good in them. To my many cousins and relatives, I thank you for your support and encouragement over the years. To my grandfathers, of which only one I knew, Pa as he was called gave me a sense of pride in his ability to survive. Grand Pa Henry was a source of strength as told by my dad, a true "John Henry " of a man.

To my extended T family, thank you for your support over the 25 years I dare not mention all by name for fear of missing anyone. To Jim Ellison, thank you for taking this ride with me and making this book a reality.

INTRODUCTION

There is a simple genesis behind my desire to write this book. It starts with an elderly man named James Hughes, a white man. My wife Judith, who's an educator and does GED testing on weekends, worked with Mr. Hughes and she often talked about him and told me what a pleasant and intelligent man he was. When she mentioned his full name I told her that my grammar school principal had been James Hughes. It turned out they were one and the same. Principals and vice-principals back then had their own homerooms, and I had been in his homeroom. I did everything from standing crossing guard at the corner with my classmate and friend John Miles to handing out books and supplies when the shipments came in. I was always eager, always ready to volunteer. Mr. Hughes seemed pleased with my efforts and my frequently raised hand, but when I searched for him through the mist of many, many years I recollected a rather strict man—fair but strict.

I decided to pay Mr. Hughes a visit. He seemed happy to talk to me. We had a pleasant conversation, but it was clear that he didn't remember who I was. I was just another in a long line of students who had passed through his grade and moved on. At first it bothered me that I was a hole in his memory. He did recall certain people in my class, including the former Senator Ed Brooks' daughter, who was in my homeroom. He also remembered the outstanding star students. My meeting with Mr. Hughes got me to thinking and I made a point of talking to other educators about the kids they remembered. They were candid in telling me they remembered the top students and the star athletes, as well as the major troublemakers. My small survey caused me to ponder an interesting question. I had certainly been far from a top student or a potentially world-class athlete (I was good at sports but not great). And so not fitting into one of the above-mentioned categories, I was not remembered. Basically I was an average kid and average kids are not the stuff from which we create role models. If you go to the library or search the Internet looking for African-American role models, you're going to come up with the usual suspects: Michael Jordan, Tiger Woods, Colin Powell, Dr. Martin Luther King, Eddie Murphy and Oprah Winfrey. When I was in high school, the principal African-American role models were Muhammad Ali, Malcolm X and Dr. Martin Luther King. You will find no Joe Average in the mix, either then or now—Joe Average who works hard, pays his taxes, honors his family, and struggles to save for his children's education. There are plenty of us out there, but the James Hughes's of the world don't remember us and never cite us or our virtues when setting up examples for other kids to follow.

Once I had met this dignified old grammar school principal who couldn't quite place me, I knew I had to write a book that speaks to the average person—black, white, woman or man. As Joe Average I accomplished a great deal—in my professional career. I served as General Manger/CEO for one of the largest businesses in all of Massachusetts, the Massachusetts Bay Transportation Authority for nearly five years, employing 6,500 people and servicing more than 1.2 million riders in 178 cities and towns. Prior to this I worked at this Authority for 20 years holding over 20 positions during my tenure. But there is nothing lofty about me, either in my speech or ideas. All I did was work hard and try to do my best. Of course, there was some luck involved, good timing and great people. Other than the fact that I now have a platform that allows me to talk to others, I am like you—and you and you.

Let's face it—those with average gifts have to try harder than others do. If you're also black, you're going to have to fight even harder for a fair shot in society. We are more likely than others to get passed over. Most of us go through the system not causing any trouble but not shining, either, and if we do cause trouble, we're stigmatized because in many people's minds, just being a black person means trouble. This is a truth we have to live with every day of our lives. Many black kids feel a secret sense of failure because their role models are sports and music icons and they know they can never live up to those large dreams. A lot of them buy $200 Nikes with money they can ill afford to spend on shoes, feeling that a gleaming pair of Nikes will give them a little piece of the dream. But they will never be able to jump, shoot or pass like Michael Jordan or entertain millions like Eddie Murphy or fill a football stadium like Snoop Dog. But so what? They aren't realistic role models anyway. They are the stuff of fantasy. These kids must be given a chance to learn that there are role models they can aspire to with a real chance of measuring up.

This, then, is the story of an average man who took advantage of every break along the way. It is a story of fun times and bad times. It is a lesson in struggle. It is a lesson in being black in America. But it is also a lesson in hope. Of the hundreds of stories, these are just a few; they are meant to give the reader a small insight in this 25 year history. I would be honored if you'd join me on this transit trip from the bus garage to the board room. Sometimes it's a bumpy ride...but it's my journey nevertheless.

THE EARLY DAYS

You may wonder how a black kid from Roxbury inner city of Boston, who never stood out at anything, ended up General Manager of the Massachusetts Bay Transportation Authority (from now on I'll refer to it either as the Authority or the T). This book may provide an answer, but a piece of the reason may have to do with my two fathers-in-law, both of whom worked for the Authority. Lenny Coley, my wife Judith's father, was a head porter on the Blue Line, one of the Authority's subway lines (named Blue because it runs along the ocean). At the time he joined the Authority, head porter was probably about the best job a black man could aspire to. There were only a handful of African Americans driving trains or buses in those days. When Judith's mother remarried, I inherited a second father-in-law, Odis Spencer. Odis did manage to achieve bus driver status, and he drove buses for more than 30 years. Both men retired from the T before I became GM. The biggest break of my life happened when Lenny called me one day and told me they were hiring bus drivers. I jumped at the chance.

But before my life at the T, there was a childhood, and a glorious childhood it was! As an only child I had the full attention of my parents, Robert Sr. and Mary. They pumped me full of hope and ambition, and they made me feel that I counted. Unlike many parents, they listened to me. They gave me advice, but subtly—never in a finger-pointing way. Maybe most important of all, they helped me to know my own roots and to be comfortable with my blackness in a world populated mainly by whites. My father had encountered racial prejudice many times in the work place, and he taught me how to cope. He worked for the State Biological Laboratory for more than 37 years as the mail clerk sending out vaccines and mail all over the country.

When someone acts unfairly or irrationally, he explained, never make his problem yours. It's important to keep a psychological distance so that you can view various issues dispassionately as they arise. My father told me that each of us is a tree with our own roots. If we know this, if we honor this, it becomes much easier to make problems into solutions. He never downplayed the difficulties of being a black person competing against whites for good schooling, good jobs and good housing, but at the same time he never made excuses for bad behavior on the part of his brethren. "You have to be stronger than the white folks," he drilled into me. "You have to work harder. You have to raise your pain threshold. Nothing worth having is ever going to be given to you for nothing. Only a fool carries a gun or does drugs to escape from reality. And we did not bring you into this world to be any kind of fool." My father lives as he taught. I was raised in a multigenerational household. My grandmother lived with us all my life. A son taking care of his mother was extremely honorable. "Nana" as she was called was a remarkable women, she died at the age we believe to be over 100. We don't know because history of births in the south were kept in bibles and if it was lost or destroyed so went the record. I have fond memories of Saturday night preparations for Sunday's dinner. Nana baking bread, preparing the chicken, collard greens, rice and gravy, telling stories of her life as a child, with her mother who was a slave, but she was born free and was extremely proud of that fact. From Society Hill, South Carolina, she would recount her life during that time. I can still hear her singing her favorite spiritual: "His Eyes are on the Sparrow." Sundays were right out of a movie, folks would drop by and everyone was fed, and with their stomachs full they would share their stories. As a child one was seen and not heard, so I honed my listening skills at an early age.

My earliest years were spent in Roxbury, which was at that time a quiet community, with a rather large Jewish population. There was a synagogue next door to us, and every Saturday the street was crowded with people going to temple. The neighborhood started to change during the 60s and I heard a lot of grumbling from my elders about deteriorating conditions. My mother cleaned people's homes in Dedham, an affluent suburb. She was a unique individual, well loved by everyone; my mother never bowed to adversity but somehow always found a way to rise above it. She brought up many of Dedham's children, and many of those children are still friends of mine today. I grew up with them, at least during the summers. My mother would take me with her to work, and I guess you could say that was my entry into the lives of the rich and powerful of Massachusetts society, at least from my perspective, and my first introduction to the public transportation called, at that time, the MTA, or Massachusetts Transit Authority. This was how she got to work every day. My early summers in Dedham were full of wide swaths of green grass to play on. I learned how to ride a bike and to play hockey, and understand that kids are just kids everywhere.

The first time I realized that I was "different" was when my friends went swimming at the Country Club, and one of the mothers explained that I couldn't join them. I didn't know at the time that I was excluded because I was black, but it must not have been long before I understood the meaning and impact of my color. I remember my mother talking to me in her quiet voice, explaining the almost unexplainable, soothing me, and somehow making me see that there was a light even at the end of that dark tunnel. My mother did not have a racist bone in her body. She grew up accepting people for who they were, and because of her winning personality, her great joy in living life to the fullest, people nearly always treated her well. I say "nearly always," because there were the inevitable slights given her color, some of them unconscious but no less hurtful for that.

She told me that when she went shopping, white women, on spotting her, would often take a tighter grip on their handbags. They did not see my mother—the most honest woman I've ever had the pleasure to know. They saw her color, and her color, because of their racist indoctrination, worried them that she might be a thief and it was better not to take a chance. Our culture is thickly layered with this kind of unconscious racist behavior from messages taught to people at dinner tables across America. The awful irony is that this unconscious racism was aimed, time and again, and sometimes in my presence, at one of the truly good human beings who ever lived. Seeing my mother treated badly cut to the core and was truly painful to me.

How can a son honor his mother? Well, I had my own distinctive way, which I will share with the reader with just the slightest touch of embarrassment. Since I was a small boy I had a habit of writing verse (I won't distinguish it by calling it poetry). Mostly I wrote it in secret—boys don't write verse—and most of it was about people who meant the most to me. This verse writing was a habit I have kept up throughout my life. The verse I will share with you now, written deep in adulthood, at my mother's passing is titled "Mary Elizabeth Prince"

> As I sat with my Dad, amongst family and friends,
> I thought about old times and changing trends.
> My mother was a constant in these heartfelt times.
> The one dependable force: I thank God she was mine.
> You know, from the paper man to the bus driver,
> They were all her friends.
> My mother was, to all, a walking U.N.
> When Alexander Graham Bell invented the phone,
> He was thinking of Mary, so she'd never be alone.
> In the past several years, we've shed too many tears.
> So, I have one small plea of those who were closest to me
> To Nana, Aunt Charlotte, Ollie, Herbie and Aunt Fran,
> Take good care of my Mom, for I know its God's plan"

Maybe it has to do with my mother's experiences, but when I go shopping I always were a suit and a tie. If I wear sneakers and jeans like the white guy shopping in the same store, I'm treated like a bum; whereas. he's simply a white guy wearing sneakers and jeans—casual weekend attire for the pale skinned nation. The clerk is likely to treat us differently. The ultimate insult is when the clerk tells me that an item is not on sale. That is the moment when the rage can kick in and I want to leap over the counter and strangle him or her. I'm afraid my answer to this kind of treatment is to wildly overspend.

My father always responded very differently. He accepted the slights as the foolishness and sickness of the white race and then shrugged and went about his business. He was a stoical man and had little to say about the racist world in which he was forced to work. He gave no quarter and expected none. I believe I am a true mixture of both my parents.

My first experience with the importance of color took place when we moved to Hyde Park, a section of Boston that abuts the suburb of Dedham. I am quite dark, and I remember walking to the bus stop soon after we moved in and the white kids kept staring at me. A little girl, clutching her book bag to her chest, couldn't keep her eyes off me. It was as though she had never seen a black person before in her life. I was not used to people looking at me in such a wide-eyed, intent way. It made me want to say *"boo!"* hoping she would drop her books and run for her life. I thought, how ignorant can you be, girl? Peel the skin away, my mother used to tell me, and we're all the same inside. It was hard at first, but I learned to accept the variety of looks cast my way—wary, fearful, ignorant, angry, whatever.

My desire to absorb learning came from my mother, just as my desire to be a man among men was the legacy from my father. By the time I was old enough to earn money by washing cars, shoveling snow and mowing lawns, I already believed in the adage, "If you talk the talk, you'd better be ready to walk the walk." Never promise what you can't accomplish, and when you start a project make sure you finish it. "Don't let anybody ever tell you what you can't do," my father told me. "Never let them limit you." In my father's world nobody was afraid to work. He wrote off the complainers, the excuse makers, the idle hands. They were not part of his orbit.

One of my distinguishing characteristics—another legacy from my father—is that I'm a "finisher." I like to complete tasks according to a set schedule or ahead of schedule if possible. You can spoil projects by sitting on them too long. As a kid I took on all kinds of jobs, including working on a construction gang operating an air drill. I gave each job my best shot. My conscience (my parents sitting right there in my mind observing me) wouldn't allow me to do less than my best. It was clear to me at a very early age that nothing short of superior results was expected of me. I took that urge for perfection through my entire career, except for schooling. I was never more than a fair student, which may have hurt my mother inwardly, but she was a great enough parent never to show her disappointment in me.

After my parents, the biggest influence on my early years was an older woman by the name of Yvonne Matthews. I remember her from the time I was six or seven years old. She was a good friend of my parents and she lived on the third floor of our multi-family house in Roxbury. She soon became like a second parent to me. It's not only your own parents who can mentor you as a child. In fact, in my experience, it's more often a family friend or a teacher or a new friend you make in high school or your first employer. Mrs. Matthews gave me my first real paying job, she was the Chief Dietician at the Lemuel Shattuck hospital, and a graduate of Tuskegee Institute in Alabama. The job was in transportation. So I guess the statement, "as the twig is bent so grows the tree," is correct. I transported patients to appointments and X-rays, delivering specimens to labs and transferring patients by ambulance. I was involved in just about anything that required movement from one place to another.

Mrs. Matthews also had a major impact on my personality. I was a pretty quiet child, reluctant to assert myself, and she gave me the courage to talk about what I hoped to accomplish when I grew up. She is a major reason why I attended Tuskegee. Under her tutelage and gentle patience, I began to develop an even stronger sense of self-worth than my parents had instilled in me. They were my parents, after all. They had to consider me special, didn't they? When I came to realize that this wise older woman believed in me, I felt a new surge of self-confidence. I was just a kid, but she made me feel I had something to offer the world. She impressed on me, through colorful anecdotes involving her own experiences, that life wasn't going to be smooth sailing for a young African-American male. She gave me advice that backed up what my father had already told me. I would have to work ten times harder than my white counterparts because there weren't going to be many breaks for me along the way. When that lesson is drilled into you again and again growing up, you begin to understand that whatever you decide to do with your life, you'd better prepare yourself carefully and give it your all. That was her philosophy. Mrs. Matthews takes up much room in my heart.

After high school, I attended an all-black university in the south—Tuskegee Institute. For the first time in my life, I felt comfortable. Yes, I was in the south, but I was among my own people; there were no critical eyes constantly stripping me naked. Let me be clear on one thing before we go any further: I love the United States of America. I think it's the greatest country on earth, and I think it could be even greater than it is. My criticism of my country grows out of my love for what it is and all the things it could become—it could be a level playing field for the poor, a haven for all races, and a truly democratic society. I also love Boston. I grew up here, after all, but I never felt comfortable as a young man. I was too visible in the eyes of the majority. I always felt that the title of Ralph Ellison's novel, *Invisible Man*, was a misnomer. We blacks are all *too* visible—black specks in a pool of whiteness. The radar is always on us, and because of that I have taught myself to be a listener, a trait that stood me in good stead during my 25 years at the Authority. [I think the phrase you were looking for was "stood me in good stead," but you don't have to use it the way I changed it.]

My ability to listen proved a great help when I became General Manager and had to attend more meetings than I care to remember. I noticed that many folks talked far too much and seemed to have taken their eyes off our particular ball, which was moving over 1.2 million people efficiently and safely. Were they trying to impress me? Did they have something worthwhile to contribute under all that verbiage? I sat on many panels with politicians, and when I talked to them they didn't hear me but were just waiting for me to draw a breath so they could resume their own monologue. I noticed that it was all about them and their constituents, and if there wasn't a vote there somewhere they were not interested. In contrast, young people are perhaps the most interesting people to listen to. I am convinced that when it comes to honesty and passion, the young have it all over the old; they have not yet developed protective shields against simple truths, devious ways of slicing and dicing the truth. I believe that the young can spot a phony a mile away. If you really care about the young, and listen to them very, very carefully, they are willing to tell you exactly what they think and feel. And if you talk to them without any "B. S"., they have not lost the capacity to listen.

My wife Judith is also a listener. She never speaks until she has something to say, and that something is always worth waiting for and listening to. I should add that she has been a powerful force in my life—as powerful as my parents and Yvonne Matthews. She has never stopped striving to educate herself, to absorb the knowledge of the world's great minds—the philosophers, the educators, the men and women of science, all while bringing up two children. She has been going to school since I've known her, and given her example, I have happily forced myself to absorb more book knowledge. I wanted to—and still strive to— make her proud of me to begin to equal the immense pride I had—and will always have—in her.

THE BUS DRIVER

I guess it was inevitable that I would end up at the Authority, given my two fathers-in-law, Lenny Coley and Odis Spencer. They liked the work and didn't feel I could do better at anything else in a racially driven city like Boston. By the time I joined, on November 8, 1976, the T was hiring more blacks and many of them were drivers. For the first 90 days I was a probationary employee struggling to help support my parents, and my biggest concern was survival. I had never driven anything larger than a Volkswagen, and now suddenly I was maneuvering a forty-foot piece of equipment through the streets of Boston where drivers were basically anarchists when they were behind the wheel. I was satisfied with the job and proud of it. It was challenging to be given the responsibility for transporting 8,200 riders each day, and it was also challenging to find my way around the streets of Boston that were unfamiliar to me. Luckily, though, I was a quick learner.

I began by driving out of Quincy Massachusetts, a suburb of Boston. When I came on the job, school busing to achieve racial integration was at its height. It's no exaggeration to say that there were major problems in the early days of busing in our city, and mistakes were made. Judge Garrity, looking for a quick solution to rid the city of school segregation, gave Charles Glenn the job of drawing up a plan to desegregate across the board. Glenn had served as director of the State Education Department's Bureau of Equal Educational Opportunity. He was an Episcopalian minister who had marched in Selma and was instrumental in planning Boston's first school boycott. In other words, his heart was in the right place.

But like many idealists, he created a plan that was uncompromising. He divided the city into school districts in such a way that each school would be forced to have the "correct" number of black and white students in proportion to the population. But the plan had the feature of busing kids between neighborhoods that had become thoroughly segregated over the years, and people in many of those neighborhoods wanted to keep it that way. Forced busing on a grand scale inflamed an already uneasy racial situation. Busing children between Roxbury—my neighborhood and a predominantly African American one—and South Boston—mainly poor and predominately Irish American—became inevitable under Glenn's plan. The busing edict was put into effect quickly, not gradually, and violence was the result. The city was torn apart, with many people in South Boston throwing rocks and bottles at incoming buses of Black students and, as a bus driver in the middle of this racial cauldron, I felt the full brunt of it. Those who couldn't flee the issue of busing (I'm talking mainly of blacks and poor whites), and move to the south shore, to places like Cohasset and Duxbury where they did not have to deal with integration, were stuck where they were. Those who remained (especially the poor whites) weren't thrilled to see a black face roll up each morning driving a MBTA bus to pick up their children for the ride to school. I got some rough treatment from the kids I drove, but as long as they kept their hands off me I was fine.

THE BLIZZARD OF '78

It was an interesting period, my beginnings at the Authority. The pay was good and I was determined to work twice as hard as the next person, if that was humanly possible. But no matter how gung-ho I was, I probably would have remained a bus driver forever if it hadn't been for the blizzard of 1978. That happened during my second year on the job. The blizzard changed my life. It was a tremendous winter storm, one of the biggest Boston had ever witnessed. Several smaller storms had preceded it, building up a huge snow accumulation. For all practical purposes, the city was shut down and under martial law. The National Guard was out in full force helping to rescue people and to reduce looting. The only people who were allowed on the road were emergency personnel—doctors, firemen, the police and transit workers. I was slated to go to work in the afternoon, but figured they might need me early. I was a guy who loved his work. Every day was a new adventure.

I pulled my car out of the garage and within a few blocks was stopped by an armed National Guardsman. My explanation that I was a transit worker—he could see my uniform plain as day—cut no ice with him. His response was, "I don't care if you're Mary Poppins, put your car back in the garage."

Arguing with an armed man in the middle of a severe crisis is never a smart thing to do, so I slipped and swerved my way back into my garage. It would have been easy to give up at that point. The snow was falling thick and piling up fast. But I felt a sense of obligation; I had already called my boss and said I would be in. The only way I could get there was on foot. At the time I was living in Brookline, which is located on the western side of Boston near the Massachusetts Turnpike. Quincy was where I was to report to, some ten miles to the south of Boston. That was quite a walk in blizzard conditions.

It was eerie out there as I trudged along, cocooned in a white world. Nothing was moving. The cars were now small white foothills along the curbs. The level of silence was deep. It was as though Boston, usually so loud and boisterous, had taken a deep breath, closed its eyes and was meditating. The only sound I heard was snow crunching under my feet as I slowly made my way south. The only images that stood out in my mind were my black prints in the snow. I passed an occasional fire truck, a snow scraper, a cop car—but they were few and far between. When I finally reached my destination some five hours later, my supervisor said, "What the hell are you doing here, Bob? You must be brain damaged." He never showed a whole lot of emotion, but I could tell he was glad I'd shown up. He was down to a skeleton crew, which meant basically that he had a couple of other drivers besides me.

I took a minute to thaw out, swallowed a cup of coffee, then grabbed a bus and headed out to Quincy Center where I picked up shovelers and returned them to their homes. By the time I finally got back home, it was nearly midnight.

It seemed that this unusual workday of mine became a piece of T folklore. Evidently some of the upper-echelon folks were mightily impressed, though I gave my winter outing little thought at the time. I just felt it was important to do my job. My father's motto, which he had pounded into me since childhood, was to do a job right. Never leave it half finished. Give it all you have, then a little extra. Earn every penny of the dollar you're paid and never do the job for money alone but for your sense of pride and your concept of the person you are. I love my father and respect the lessons he taught me.

Even though I was one of the new kids on the block, right on the bottom rung of the T, I already sensed a mission growing inside me. As T employees, we were charged with the responsibility of moving people and making sure that public transportation ran the very best it could even under the worst of conditions. My decision to get to work when others didn't or couldn't seem to have a ripple effect, I learned later that word about me—this young black bus driver—reached up the ladder of the MBTA. I wouldn't go so far as to say this single small example of devotion to duty catapulted me to higher levels, but I began to sense that folks were no longer looking at me in quite the same way. I became just a little more visible in ways that had nothing to do with my color. Not long after that extraordinary blizzard, my supervisor in the bus division made calls "upstairs" to say this is a guy to keep your eye on. A few months later I bid for another job down into the subway system.

To my mind, I hadn't done anything all that unusual. I hadn't worked a miracle. There were many incidents of men and women who worked for the authority that had made extraordinary sacrifices during that time. In fact, I hadn't done anything anybody couldn't have done once they set their mind to it. I walked ten miles through a blizzard to help out when I could have stayed home and nobody would have thought the worse of me, but I chose not to do that. I chose instead to accept a day of freezing, some inconvenience and a whole lot of bone-tiredness from putting in an 18-hour day. But what was the big deal? I was healthy and in my 20s. Any healthy young person could have done what I did. It's all a matter of motivation and attitude, two words I heard a lot about from my parents and Mrs. Matthews growing up. A wise man once said that if you're a street cleaner, be the best street cleaner in the world. Take pride in what you do. Make your job count for something. Make your street the cleanest street in the town where you live.

SUMO MAN

During those early days at the T, race was a hot button issue, even hotter than it is today. I was driving buses during the height of busing in Boston, and busing in my town was about as popular as the New York Yankees. As I mentioned, I was working out of Quincy, a tough working class neighborhood south of Boston, and nobody was exactly rolling out the welcome wagon for me. When people saw my black face they thought dark thoughts of busing, agitation, change, and a whole bunch of negatives. As a junior person in the garage I got the ugly routes, the places you wouldn't want to visit even in the daytime. One of the worst areas of all was German Town/Houghs Neck, a place full of kids who wanted to lay a hurt on me the minute they spotted my color. When I pulled up, teenagers would throw things at the bus—stones, oranges, eggs, battered baseballs—and then start screaming "Nigger! Nigger! Nigger!" Some of the older, more understanding bus passengers would ask me how I could take the abuse and keep my cool. I explained that I refused to give them the satisfaction of reacting to their taunts, but I didn't forget either. I kept a tally book and I made plans.

One day, one of those hoodlums would be standing at a bus stop in the pouring rain—and what do you know? I wouldn't see him standing there. He would wave his arms and I would just keep on rolling. But that was fantasy. My job was to pick up passengers and that is what I did-pick up everyone, even the knuckleheads. I had a more practical plan in mind.

I had been working the German Town Houghs/Neck route for about a month when I took a group of kids on a school trip. They were unruly, running up and down the aisle throwing spitballs and shouting the "N" word loud enough for me to hear. When they kept it up I stopped the bus. I turned to them and said I was going to drive them to Grove Hall and drop them off. Grove Hall was a predominantly black area in Boston, and the kids there looked no more kindly on whites than the German Town Houghs/Neck kids looked on blacks. "If you want to carry on and call me names," I told them, "let me take you to a place where you can chant nigger and really get yourself some action."

"There's a 40-to-one situation here," I explained, never once raising my voice. "There are all of you and there's just one of me. But when I let you off at Grove Hall, the odds are going to even up fast."

The bus went silent at that point. They probably thought I was crazy. That's what I wanted them to think. Those were poor kids, many of their parents were unemployed. I'm sure they had been indoctrinated against forced busing—and here was this big black dude wearing a uniform of authority and threatening them with a trip to their version of Hell. As far as I was concerned, I was there to operate the equipment and not to get personal, just so long as they didn't spit on me or lay a hand on me. I'm a pretty big guy—two-fifty, with muscles—and if you decide to get physical you'd better be carrying a brick or a bat.

Standing up to those kids, and yet not bullying them or returning their insults with some choice ones of my own, began to shift the attitude in the bus. A few of them even began to speak to me, acknowledging by that act that I might actually be a fellow human being. One kid began calling me "sumo man," which I took as a compliment and a sign of at least faint affection. P.S.: I never did have to drive them to Grove Hall.

INCIDENT AT THE BUS GARAGE

In the T itself, people weren't wheeling out the welcome wagon either. There was talk of reaching out to do more minority hiring and to institute a more vigorous promotion policy, but the few blacks employed by the Authority when I started out were Operators and rarely rose above that rank. I never felt accepted at the Quincy Bus Garage and kept pretty much to myself. You were supposed to arrive at the job 10 minutes early, and being a freak for punctuality I would drive up 30 to 40 minutes before starting time and sit in my car listening to the radio until it was time to do the pullout. Then I would check with the Inspector, who was the person in charge, sign for the bus, pick it up and take off. I didn't see any point in trying to interact with folks who didn't want me there in the first place. For me, it was all about my bus and the people I carried. It was all about picking them up on time and delivering them where they were going on time. Damned if I would lose sight of that. The other Operators could go their way and I would go mine. We weren't going to be taking any strolls on the beach together. I wasn't going to be invited home to dinner to meet the wife and kids. And I was cool with that. The few blacks that were hired around the time I was and worked out of areas like Quincy didn't last long, mainly because Quincy was considered a senior rated garage; those who were new were often bumped out by a senior person. No question, Quincy was a tough gig for a black man; it gets really chilly if people don't approve of the color of your skin. It didn't much matter to me if they liked me or not and there was no way I was going to make their problem mine. I kept my mouth shut, did my job, and then went home. You do bond with those whom you break in with, and seven of us came on together and went to Quincy. Being junior in a senior environment is nerve racking.

During my days in Quincy, I took the test and became a spare Starter, sometimes filled in as a spare desk starter, assigning work to the other Operators. One night, the Supervisor told me that he wanted me to see a particular individual the minute he got off his route. The Supervisor laboriously wrote out his instructions, perhaps assuming that I must have a limited attention span. When I spotted the driver, I called him to the window and told him the Supervisor wanted to see him pronto. Well, he went ballistic on me. Screaming, spittle spraying from his mouth, he warned me never to bother him or speak to him again on his break. If there had not been a grate separating us, I might have thrown my career away then and there and strangled him. What was worse, when the Supervisor approached the driver, the guy's temper suddenly vanished and he was all smiles and smarmy cooperation.

I sat there and stewed for a while, then decided to meet with the man in private. I cornered him in the garage and told him that if he ever acted that way again, berating me in front of others, I would have him up on charges. I spoke to him very quietly. Standing a respectful, non-threatening distance from him I said, "We both work for the T. We're both drivers. As far as I'm concerned we're equals. You don't have to like me, but I am going to insist that you treat me like an equal while we're on the job." I added, still very quietly, "If you have other issues, we can settle those away from here, out of uniform. You name the place and the time." After that, there were no more issues. He kept his distance from me.

WHAT GOES AROUND COMES AROUND

"The subway is the place to be, son." Those words of wisdom were drummed into me by my father-in-law, Lenny Coley, from the moment I joined the T. No man knew the inner workings of the organization better than he did. When I had a chance to bid down and become a part of the subway system, I grabbed it. Lenny Coley was right, as always. I was in for a great experience.

I had had a lot of fun driving buses, but I knew that it was time to move on. I have to explain that within the MBTA surface operations (Bus Operations) and Rapid Transit (train operations) are two separate divisions, so one cannot get from bus to trains without a unique set of circumstances occurring. One of those is the extension of a train line that takes work away from the buses. This opportunity arrived in 1978. I had a discussion with the union barn captain about giving up two years of seniority at the T; anytime you get a new job, you go to the bottom of the seniority list, and seniority is important for vacation options and schedules you pick for work. He said, "in time, it won't matter." If you didn't take opportunities when they were offered to you, they might never be offered to you again. This turned out to be great advice. Even as a rookie driver, I had been aware of opportunities opening up at the T for guys like me. And by "guys like me" I mean people who were willing to keep their noses clean and close to the grindstone. You could climb the ladder if you had your heart set on it and were willing to give just a little more than you thought you had in you. My goal from the beginning was never to be satisfied with one position if there was another, better one up ahead. Over the next 25 years, I held more than 20 jobs.

When I moved underground and began to work on the Blue Line, which carries passengers from Boston to the North Shore, I was thrilled. I figured I had done my time on the South Shore (Quincy) and it was high time to see what was happening in another part of the Authority. The only hitch was that moving underground meant losing my "rating," or, in layman's terms, it meant starting over. People on the Subway side who were hired after me were now senior to me, but I did it anyway.

One afternoon, not long after I became an Inspector, I got a radio call about trouble brewing at Maverick Station, the station before Aquarium. As the train approached, I jumped on board. It's worth noting here that Inspectors were badged police on the Property only, and although they did have the power to arrest they did not carry guns. I approached a group of kids who were causing a major disturbance. I was able to get them off the train, line them up against the wall and wait for the transit police. A few minutes' later, two white officers arrived. As it turned out, one of the officers lived in the neighborhood and he began to chew the kids out big time, a down-with-it neighborhood tongue-lashing. I felt good about that because he had grown up with those kids and could serve as a role model for them.

At least that's what I thought, but then he blew it. "You boys brought me all the way over to East Boston," he yelled. "You drag me through the tunnel, when I could be in Roxbury chasing niggers and real crooks."

Suddenly it grew very quiet on that platform. The kids didn't know where to look or what to do, and a couple of them shot a quick glance at me, gauging my reaction. The transit cop's partner's cigarette drooped off his lips and nearly burned his goatee. An eternity of time seemed to pass as the cop realized what he'd said and labored to adjust his attitude. Finally, he turned to me with a large, cheesy grin and said, "Well, there are white niggers too, you know what I mean?"

"I know what you mean," I said, as rage struggled with my parents' message ringing in my ear to not let someone else's problem (racism) become mine.

He was unthinkingly practicing the kind of systemic racism that went on and continues to go on not only in Boston, a fertile field for it, but everywhere in this nation. He was just more up front in voicing the prevailing sentiments. It's laughable to me that just because I finally became General Manager of the Authority there were those who actually believed I could cure our racial ills. The problem—the underlying rot—is everywhere, in every big city, in every hamlet throughout the land. In fundamental ways this country still suffers the blight of its slave-master past.

There is an old saying that says, what goes around comes around. Shortly after I became General Manager we had a fatality out in the northern part of the state. I needed a police escort to get me there, and a cruiser was sent around. I went downstairs and climbed in the cruiser with a press person, and surprise of surprises, next to the driver was the very same transit cop who had had that conversation with those kids nearly 20 years earlier. Needless to say, the ride for him was on the endless side. His body language and behavior suggested that the incident still lived in him as it did in me. Not a word of what had taken place was exchanged between us. But we both knew what we knew. Had he changed his views in those 20 years? I have no way of knowing. Had I changed? A little, at least. I am more tolerant about the state of humankind than I once was, not as quick to take offense and to blame. We are all flawed, and yet we have to find workable ways to live together. That cop, who I learned retired a few months later, will never invite me to his house, nor will I invite him to mine. I believe that as humans we need to find a way within ourselves to walk forward in peace. A little bit of progress is all we can ever hope for. [By deleting "which" I have made the previous sentence a sentence. As it was, the "which" was begging for more...something.] I recognize and appreciate that change happens incrementally and over time.

This belief in the possible is tied to our self-esteem. When I was growing up in the 60s I'd never heard of self-esteem. I was taught to brush my teeth, shower every day, wear clean clothes and be respectful to my elders. I was taught that God loves all human beings equally, and that different folks have different Gods. I was taught that if I worked hard in school and didn't cheat and lie, I would somehow be rewarded. I was taught that my black skin was as good as—*but no better than*—any other skin color. I now believe that all the above lessons in being civilized amounted to a series of attitudes and beliefs that would automatically imbue me with self-esteem.

But when I entered the world outside my close-knit family I was tested—tested by the people I worked with, the kids on the bus, by indifference, apathy, covert prejudice and downright discrimination. The thing I now called self-esteem was severely tested. For a while I was an angry young man, and maybe I was a little too willing to see myself as others saw me. Slowly, though, I came to a realization of what I had been given as a child. My parents had mentored me on important issues; they had believed in me. They had not sent me out into the world with a set of false hopes, platitudes and phony values. They had given me a compass to guide me through the tough times. They had never led me to believe that success should be pursued at the expense of honesty and loyalty and pride. And at the same time, they taught me to stand up for myself and for what I was convinced were the right things to do in any situation. I must say though in all honesty I am a complicated person, and I compartmentalize issues and feelings. This at times made life difficult, because what do you do when the compartment is full?

CODE 2

After bidding over to the subway division, I discovered that driving trains was just as big a bang as driving buses. I loved it! It's a rush operating something that big that carries up to 1,000 passengers. I would like to tell you that my time on the front end of a train was without issue and that I was a model operator, but that would be untrue. I made mistakes as everyone does but I never made them twice. I then took the Inspectors' exam and passed, after which, in short order, I took a number of other tests and was promoted. Prior to becoming an Inspector there was the proverbial ladder to climb, Collector (who sells tokens to access the system), Train Guard (who opens and closes train doors), Motorman (who drives the train), and Starter. Inspector was a sort of "Jack of all Trades" position. I was responsible for police actions, train repairs, fires and the general assistance of passengers. I also monitored all of the employees in the stations in my jurisdiction. From there I moved up to Chief Inspector and then to Train Starter. A Train Starter manages the payroll, handles the work assignments, issues checks, makes sure the trains run on time, and adjusts the schedules accordingly. After that, there was an opening for a Dispatcher working in the Operations Control Center (OCC). I wanted that promotion so bad I could taste it, and with the help of Mike Anderson, who was working in the OCC, and some excellent test scores, I landed the job. It's no exaggeration to say that Dispatcher is the toughest job in the T because you really don't control anything in the control center. Control is a misnomer. You are sitting in a dark room and don't get to see what the problem is. You have to rely on the information coming in over the radio from the Motorperson. You give directions and pray to God that people pay attention and do the right thing. Others call you for help during times of need and there is plenty of pressure on you to make sure you direct the proper personnel to the locations where they're needed and in a timely fashion. If you don't, someone is sure to have your head. Basically, the Dispatcher is a trouble shooter for anything that can and ultimately does go wrong, from fires to police actions to train derailments. The Dispatcher is the first person to make decisions when a problem rears its head, and because each subway line has its own distinct "personality," I had to be trained on all three lines so I would know what to do when a problem arose. Anything that has to do with the way the Authority functions underground—anything that goes wrong—comes through the operations control center and can come back to haunt you. I loved the challenge.

One of the most traumatic moments in all my years at the Authority was when a Motorman called in from the Orange Line on a Sunday, late in the afternoon, and said he had a Code 2. A Code 2 signals that there is a person under a vehicle. The Motorman was between Sullivan Station and Community College, which is in the northern section of Boston. When he keyed up his mike I could hear a baby screaming through the radio. The Motorman was upset and tearful. He said, "No way am I going out and look at this." "Don't do anything," I said. "Secure your train." I tried to remain as calm as I could and told him that help was on the way. I began to dispatch fire and police and then a supervisor to the location. And each time the Motorman keyed up the mike I could hear that child screaming under the train. As it turned out, a Vietnamese woman had missed her stop and had decided she would walk the rest of the way to the next station along a narrow pathway. She fell and was struck by the train and killed. Her child, who was clutched tightly in her arms, somehow managed to survive. I immediately began to second-guess myself: Maybe I could have gotten help to the location faster. If we could have gotten to the woman sooner she might have lived. The psychological toll on the survivor can be punishing.

One day on the Orange Line, three years later, I ran into the Motorman again. He introduced himself and said, "You know, I had to go to a psychiatrist after that woman died on the tracks. My life was a mess—nightmares and sleepless nights." He regarded me with hostility and added, "This may sound strange, but I was pissed off at you. I had no right to be, but I was. You were so calm about a situation that was so drastic." I listened to him and then said, "You'll never know how much that incident bothered me. There was no way I could let you know what I was feeling. If I had I wouldn't have been doing my job. Then we'd both have been basket cases and nothing would have been done."]I told him there was no point in both of us screaming and falling apart. But that day stayed with me for a long time, and in fact it never really left me. The truth be known, for a long time I could still hear the baby's cries. It got so bad with the lack of sleep I confided in my childhood friend Steve who said he could give me the number of a physiologist who could help me relax but I had to call right then and make an appointment. He knew that I would never do this without an ultimatum. Well I did and learned not only progressive relaxation techniques but also self hypnosis, which came in very handy later on. I've only had a couple of times at the T where I had trouble coping emotionally and that was one of them.

CLIMBING THE T LADDER

I held many more positions between the time of that particular incident and my five years as General Manager that began in 1997. I moved on from Dispatcher to Night Superintendent. This was my first real "suit and tie" position. It was also a traveling position. I would be contacted by the Dispatcher to go wherever a problem was occurring. I had control of Rapid Transit. Every night I would supervise the rush hour and monitor maintenance and operations. It was my responsibility to make sure the appropriate crews were in place and that the service was moving accordingly. That was the position I liked most of all up to that point in my career. As the Night Superintendent I was the man in charge. Having worked underground for so long I had truly earned my nickname—The Prince of Darkness. From Night Superintendent I moved on to become Deputy Superintendent of Rail Lines, and for the first time in years worked in daylight again. By then my reputation had preceded me; no test was needed for the job. I was hand picked. I was now on the inside, one of "the boys," and one of the very few minorities on a senior level. It took some time getting used to working in the daytime, but the job had its fascinations. This was where I learned how to write up discharges, diversions, and special orders. I stayed in this position for five years. When the Acting General Manager JR, a young man from South Boston who rose up through the T ranks, reached out for me to become his Special Assistant, I was ready for the challenge, which included the purchase of better ties and jackets.

Jim was an old friend at the T, and the launching pad for everything that followed for me. I had known him for years. He told me that he needed my operations expertise as well as my loyalty. I handled a lot of delicate political situations during my time with him. He taught me everything about politics, which was something new to me and a world apart from operations. I also got more involved in the administrative side of the business. Jim was such a good friend that he prompted one of my special verses of praise and good fellowship penned for a roast in honor of Jim when he was leaving the T. At the risk of filling the room full of laughter, I am going to set it down here word for word.

Well, I've called him slick
I've called him sly
I've never called him slim
'cause that would be a lie.

From swinging a track hammer on an E&M crew
To deputy GM—my, what we've been through!
But now that I know the die has been cast
I'd like to talk a little about this man's past.
The Southie lad made a hell of a sight
While the bodies were buried as he held the light.
Now I know there are subjects that are strictly taboo,
But he's leaving the T, so what can he do!
Jim's athletic ability is known far and wide;
I'll give you one example and let the rest ride.
It was a half court pass during a pick up game
Where the flash speed of Rooney made all of us ashamed.
The nickname slow turtle would be most appropos:
He had plenty of get up...he just had no go!
In Bermuda where he was king of the limbo,
He bought round after round (thank God for ole Jimbo)
The T stories are many, but none can be told.
We swore on the Bible we'd stand by the code,
And when asked of the past the answer is clear:
"If I tell you I'll have to kill you for what you would hear."
Now I've refrained from abuse and being overly crass,
Mainly 'cause Jim's on the list and he gets to go last.
So let's say that we'll bring this poem to an end.
You call him Jim Rooney.....I call him my friend.

Jim's reaching out to me and giving me opportunity proved my theory about most people being good people. Here he was a man from South Boston and one from Roxbury who came together to lead the nation's first subway system.

When John Haley became General Manager a few months later, he made me Acting Director of EEO (Equal Employment Opportunity) rather than keep me on as his Special Assistant. Within three months, though, I was back with Haley, who, in short order, had reorganized the Authority. I was named Assistant General Manager for Human Resources. He needed someone who understood the operational needs of the T in this totally non-operational position. The job was a big one. I was in charge of Human Resources, Labor Relations, the MBTA Clinic, and Benefits and Compensation. It was not the greatest fit in the world for me, but if they needed me and needed what I had to bring to the table, I was more than willing to give it my best shot. And I did just that, sensing that this was not the end of the story for me. This part of my journey was not without the help, understanding and support from a number of department heads and their staff.

One person who, although small in size, was large in stature was Linda, my very first Chief of Staff. We spent countless hours dealing with internal and external politics surrounding jobs and placements an area of remarkable sensitivity.

THE KITCHEN CABINET

My initial internal group was comprised of fellow colleagues in various areas throughout the Authority. Ray Diggs from Operations, Gwen Dillday from EEO, Bill Mumford from Employment, Lucy Shorter from Marketing, and Beverly Harris also from Employment, were the core group that got expanded as the years passed. When you think of survival I have to reinforce that you cannot do it alone. We were all African Americans and each other's sanity check. We would hold meetings periodically for coffee and to discuss the inner workings of the T. Opportunities and personal coping strategies were topics, but the camaraderie was most important; it was how we survived many hostile experiences.

THE BOB & RAY SHOW

Raymond Diggs Sr. and I had been friends and colleagues for many years; he was an ear that listened, advisor when needed, and a "dope slap "when necessary. Going to schools to tell students about the opportunities in transportation before there were programs was one of our initial goals. We continued this process through our many years at the Authority.

A couple of years later the "Conference of Minority Transportation Officials" (COMTO) was brought to Boston. At a time when an organization was needed to advocate and communicate with minorities in transportation, I was glad finally that an organization focused on my needs was here. I became involved in the mid 80's with COMTO, which allowed me to reach others in the industry outside the MBTA. I met pioneers in the industry who continued with what Rosa Parks started. A friend and official once said during a speech that, "because she (Rosa Parks) sat where she sat, I now stand where I stand," a legacy lest we forget from whence we came. The Carmens, Beverlys, Shirleys, Bobbys, Gordons, Franks, Pauls, Wills, Johns and Deans to name a few, all pioneers in their own right helped mold the transit industry and pave the way for the Bob Princes to be given opportunity.

ENTER JACK

I knew and was touched by so many people during my 25 years at the Authority—by people who cared for me regardless of, or in spite of, or because of, my race, height, disposition or shockingly good looks. (That's an example of the Bob Prince attempt at humor.) These folks I'm referring to—far too many to count—are better known as my dear friends. When I met them, they were disguised as fellow T colleagues. I didn't have any idea that they would become not only crucial to my success as General Manager but close members of my personal circle.

Perhaps the foremost among them was Jack Killgoar. I remember as though it were yesterday a fellow worker, Mike Francis, telling me he'd heard through the grapevine that I was about to get a phone call from the Superintendent's office. The Deputy Superintendent position was about to open up, and I was on the short list of those being considered for the job. Shortly after that, I was called in to meet Jack. At first glance we seemed to be the total opposite of each other. I am a black man, he is a white man. I am tall and heavy, he is short and slim. He is a high strung individual, I am calm. The differences go on and on, and those differences were obvious the day I met him, and they gave me some pause. If we were all that different from each other, why would he pick me, of all people, to be his Deputy Superintendent?

At the beginning of the interview I said to him, "To quote Shakespeare, some people are born great, some people achieve greatness, and some people have greatness thrust upon them." I paused and added, "If you feel I've been thrust on you then let's not have this conversation because I'm happy at what I'm doing now." He assured me that wasn't the case and that, as Superintendent, he had actually selected me. "I didn't need suggestions from anybody," he said. "I've been following your career at the T."

"If you picked me just because I'm black I don't want to be here."

He listened, nodded, and then responded with equal candor. "Race has nothing to do with it, Bob. You work hard and you're smart and honest. Don't think I'm doing you any favors. I promise to work your butt off." He grinned. "I'll have you begging for mercy."

"And if I don't measure up?"

"You'll be gone. Doesn't matter what color you are."

I knew right then that we were on a level playing field. He needed me as much as I needed him. In no time at all he was not only my office mate but my mentor and, most importantly, my friend for life. Jack was by no means color blind, and neither was I. He is Irish white, and I am very definitely African black. But the beautiful thing is that color didn't matter to us at all. We had moved beyond it.

I count Jack Killgoar as one of the major mentors in my life, and I feel the impact of his intelligence and honesty every day. When I got to know him, I couldn't help but be reminded of Clark Kent and Superman. He had the somewhat academic, befuddled manner of Kent but he could morph smoothly into the Superman role when necessary. He was a little intimidating to me at first—a Dorchester kid, a graduate of Boston Latin and Boston College. This is not someone I would have ordinarily befriended, but over the years he became one of my closest friends at the T, a man I could trust implicitly. Jack taught me a large piece of what I know about transportation and probably just as much about life itself.

From the moment I went to work for him it was the "mentor" and the "mentored." Under Jack, I did everything from working with the Unions and writing reports and whatever needed to be done to satisfying the inner workings of the Rapid Transit System. He taught me all of those things and he taught me well. He always made certain I understood that whatever I did could be done even better, with greater efficiency. "Use your imagination," was his mantra. The phrase "think out of the box" had not yet been coined, but he was someone who practiced it on a daily basis.

During the period I worked with Jack, we became involved in a complex arbitration case. A woman from Labor Relations, Tricia Day, had me testify. After the testimony, one of the Union delegates became incensed about the position we'd taken and he literally jumped into my chest and started hollering. I put my hands in my pockets and stared at him, but did not back away. I was sure that at any second he was going to haul off and hit me, which might have proved interesting. Just as the guy drew back an arm, Tricia yelled out and Jack grabbed me and walked me out into the hallway. I looked at the two of them and said, "Why did you do that?" "I was afraid he was going to take a punch at you," Tricia answered." "Well, you just stopped his children from going to Harvard," Jack said with a smile. "What a lawsuit Bob would have had."

That was vintage Jack. Nothing ever rattled his cage. He was always in control. He was the guy I listened to back then and he still is to this day. From the beginning, the beauty of our relationship was that it was never about boss and employee. It was about two guys doing their level best to run transportation. We very seldom saw each other away from the T, but whenever we did we enjoyed each other's company. When people we'd known for years started to retire from the T, Jack, who wasn't much for socializing, told me that he thought he'd pass on the retirement parties. He was the kind of guy who liked to go straight home from work each night and cool out with his family. That was when I finally had a chance to mentor my mentor. "It's not just about who's retiring," I told him. "It's almost more about who's staying. We're all in this together. By showing up for a few hours and having a drink or two and a little reminiscence, you're honoring those who are leaving and those we'll still be working with." Jack got the message and started attending with me.

Years later, when I moved back to head up Operations, I was suddenly Jack's boss. Some people second-guessed our new working relationship. After all, I had once worked under him. Was this new arrangement seemly? Well, as far as Jack and I were concerned titles were only titles. He wasn't working "for" me, just as, years earlier, I had not worked "for" him. We had always just worked together, with one mission in mind. It was all about delivering service, and when it came to delivering service to the commuting public, Jack was always number one. Because he was one of the best friends I've ever had, or ever hope to have, Jack, too, was the recipient of one of my "verses" when his day came to leave the T. Here it is, in full:

I have been known at times
To converse in rhyme,
So after deep reflection
This should be no exception.
The subject this time is JRK,
Jack Killgoat to most, I've a few things to say.
When he arrived at the T, quite fresh from B.C.,
I had just had a birthday—I think I was three.
Young, energetic, suave, and debonair,
Some say at that time he even had hair.
After his rise through the ranks, knowledge being his game,
It wasn't too long before all knew his name.
With Jack it was truth, justice and the American Way.
It was like working with Clark Kent day after day.
You just knew that behind those glasses and thinning hair style
There was the man of steel, fast thinking all the while.
At arbitrations he would shine, always put to the test;
That's where I saw Superman with the red "S" on his chest.
With Jack you learned to dot every I and cross every T.
If you failed at that task after school you would be.
There are many Jack stories but my favorite I'll share:
Of his first helicopter ride, you just had to be there.
As we took off the doors and they were laid on the pad,
Jack looked at me and said "Are you stark raving mad?"

His primary concern was extremely heartfelt:
His life was being suspended by a tiny seat belt.
He questioned the copter's safety, and the pilot (what a kidder)
Told him to sit back and relax he went with low bidder.
As the chopper took off Jack had quite a grip.
I said if you want any pictures, let go of the ship.
All kidding aside, I wouldn't be where I am
If it were not for Jack Killgoar. He is quite a man.
His wit, charm and council are missed day-to-day.
This feeling is felt through the entire subway.

They say, "Reach one teach one." Jack taught me and through his example and tutelage; that is what I tried to do with others.

ENTER TRUSTED COLLEAGUES

As I mentioned earlier, I am the one and only offspring of two incredible parents, about whom I could write an entire book. They encouraged me in everything I ever tried to do. They were both absolutely honest with me, honest and fair, and they urged me to excel. My father told me that the secret to success is to do everything, even the very smallest of things, the very best you can do it. If you're cleaning a pot, make it shine. If you're mowing a lawn, make sure there are no ragged edges. If you're studying a subject in school, don't take the easy shortcuts just to get the grade, but learn what it's all about; get right there inside of it. If you don't try to do your best, the only person you're cheating is yourself.

One of my fellow colleagues would remind me often of my "only child syndrome," as she called it. She said that I was the center of my parents' universe, and maybe in some ways I was. But I don't think I suffered from that syndrome, if indeed I had such a syndrome at all. More likely I benefited from it. They made me feel humble and yet, at the same time, important. But in order to introduce Maryanne Walsh, a very special colleague, properly I must record her observation about that only child business. Maryanne—19 when she joined the T—comes from a big Irish family with an overflow of genes for charm and hard work. She joined my team when I was called up from the Deputy Superintendent position to become a Special Assistant in the General Manager's office. This call of duty was indeed a great honor for me—another step up the ladder and far beyond any height I had envisioned back in the days when I was a Bus driver.

My new office, which had been functioning as a storage room and file closet (and where Maryanne worked at the time), was situated some ways away from the then General Manager's commodious corner-space, Don't get me wrong—underneath the incredible rubble there was a desk and a door and four walls. I came in over a weekend and cleared the room of the rubble, put up some stylish pictures, plugged in a phone, and by Monday morning I had a decent space laid out for myself.

Upon Maryanne's arrival on the first Monday morning in my new position, she was surprised to see me sitting in this mess of an office, but managed to greet me with a puzzled and rather unsteady "Good morning." She went to her office, wondering who I was. In the flurry of motion and events that morning we didn't have a moment to introduce ourselves. Just before she arrived, a coworker of Maryanne's told me that if I needed pencils or pens I could go to a nearby Staples or the GM's office to scratch some up. My spirits were sinking by the moment. I had had expectations that being part of the inner "Parliament" would come with some perks, but I was being pulled back to reality in a flash. After Maryanne hung up her coat and got the 411 on what was up with the "guy sitting in the storage closet," she came over and gave me a proper welcome. She told me that if there was anything I needed to feel free to ask her. I began to feel like a human being for the first time that day.

Soon I was moved out of that office/closet and into an honest-to-God office next to the General Manager. Within weeks after that move I was asked to head up Human Resources and I needed to put together a support team. That's when *I* asked Maryanne to come along with me, and she entered the picture in a big way, creating order out of chaos. She assumed the role of Senior Manager in charge of administration and stayed as part of my team until the day I retired. Maryanne remains my friend to this day.

After spending some years on the Administration side of the T, I was given an opportunity to return to Operations as the Assistant General Manager of Subway Operations and then as Chief Operating Officer in charge of all Operations. This was like coming home for me. Managing Human Resources, Labor Relations, EEO and Benefits & Compensation had been a valuable experience, but there was nothing to compare to heading up Operations. That was where my heart was. That was where I came to rely upon a man whom I would later name as my Chief of Staff when I became General Manager of the T. His name is Mikel Oglesby and he was instrumental in forming the reorganization that was necessary for Operations. He, too, was someone I had known from way back. His family had lived a few streets from mine in Roxbury when Mikel was a child. Again, it's a small world, folks. Maybe even fewer than six degrees separate us all.

Our neighborhood in Boston—Mikel's and mine—being predominantly black, was home to many African-Americans who worked for the Authority at one time or another. Mikel's father drove a bus for the T for more than 30 years. He was proud of the Authority and extremely loyal to it and, like Maryanne's father, he encouraged his children to join the T family. Mikel started working for the T as an Analyst in Operations. He was promoted a short time later to the Budget Office, which was also located near the GM's office, within hailing distance of me. We knew each other from way back, but not many people were aware that we knew each other. His promotion to the Budget office came shortly before I got called on by the then General Manager to be Special Assistant. We never spoke much about our boyhood experiences in Roxbury, and because his family moved out when he was just a child, our views were probably different in many ways. But when he became a part of my team as an adult, it was as if we had never parted. He was a young hot shot eager to make a name for himself, and he had the goods to back his ambitions up. He shared my time as the Black General

Manager of the Authority (a first) as my Black Chief of Staff (also a first). Some people may not understand what I mean by my being "Black General Manager," or by my reference to Mikel as being my "Black Chief of Staff." Just to be clear on this point, when whites referred to us, we were "you know…the black guys, Prince and Oglesby." It was as though our functions were defined by our color. Color came before all else.

Mikel was a bright guy. We were in touch on a daily basis, and we often had to laugh at the outrageous behavior of those who didn't share our skin color. He was tough on under performers, and his jovial personality would sometimes give people a false sense of hope that when they were called into his office they would just receive a friendly reminder of what was expected of them. More often than not, they would emerge from the meeting chastened. If there was anyone who didn't suffer fools gladly, Mikel was at the head of the list.

Like Maryanne, he stayed with me until I retired.

THE FLOOD OF '96

In 1996, while I was still Chief Operating Officer, with bus, subway, light rail, commuter rail and basically everything else that carried a human being from point A to point B under my supervision, I lived through one of the worst disasters since the aforementioned blizzard of '78. The event I'm about to relate was probably more key than any other in elevating me to the top position at the T a year later. You can say the flood of October '96 was my defining moment. People don't pay as much attention to rain fall as they do to snow fall, but you better believe that the two natural forces are equal in their ability to wreak destruction. During that fall, Boston was drenched with unusually heavy rains. The Regatta, a boat race on the Charles River, and big news in Boston, was about to take place. Ordinarily during the race the river level is raised so that boats don't bottom out anywhere. The Charles is operated on floodgates so that the Metropolitan District Commission can raise or lower the river when necessary. That weekend the flooding had grown to such serious proportions that the race was threatened. And for the first time in my memory the river level actually overflowed.

After many years with the T, I had developed a sixth sense about bad things happening. There were the usual physical signs—racing pulse, soaring blood pressure, general irritability. That Sunday afternoon I was having dinner with my in-laws and my mood was jumpy. All I could think about was rain, and more rain. That night around midnight I called the operations control center to check on the conditions. The panicked voice on the other end of the phone, Maureen, led me to lace up my boots and head over to the Kenmore Station. Jack, Superintendent of Green Line Operations, met me there. Together we walked down the stairs toward the underground subway station and moved slowly along the portal. What we saw would take a James Cameron of *Titanic* fame to recreate. A few minutes after we got down inside, we heard a thunderous crash followed by a torrent of water pouring in from a basketball-size hole in the wall. It rushed with such force that by the time we made our way back to the platform the water was up to our knees.

I called the General Manager and told him he'd better make his way down on the double. From the stress in my voice he knew we were in a big mess. When he did show up about an hour and a half later, carrying a pair of little boots in his hand, we were all huddled around the Collector's booth.

"What's the problem, Bob?" he asked.

"Well, you won't have any need for those boots," I said.

He looked puzzled. "But you told me there's flooding in the portal."

"Yeah," I said, "but you'll need scuba gear."

I explained that according to the engineers, there were some 40 million gallons of water under us, rising to a height of 18 feet, from the base of the platform all the way to the ceiling on the first level. The eerie part was that the tracks were still lighted; you could look down and see a massive, illuminated body of water.

He turned to me, his jaw muscles working furiously. "Okay. What do we do now, Bob?" (I wanted to say what do you mean "we.")

"We get rid of the water," I told him.

For the next four days the Chief of Design and Construction, the Director of Subway Operations, and I never left the site except for quick food and bathroom breaks. One emergency piled on another. We had meetings with the construction and maintenance people to remove the water from the subway, and then there was the cleanup operation to coordinate after we got the water out. Once it was dry enough underground we had to reestablish the signal system by hand while keeping service running through an expanded busing operation. Believe me, putting all those pieces together was one neat trick.

It took a miracle to move that amount of water out of the system. The miracle, of course, was no miracle at all. It was simply hard work beyond the point of exhaustion. We brought in everybody to help us pump the water out, from the Army Corps of Engineers to every contractor we could beg, borrow or steal. We pumped water into all available empty spaces. Our one and only priority was to get it out of the subway. It was like Dante's Inferno down there—ladders wedged on the ceiling, the waterline up to the ceiling, people running around screaming orders. Incredibly, no one died or was even badly injured. To see the degree of effort it took for our workers to remove all the ballast (small rocks between the tracks) in the area, to wipe the stations down, to clean the rails by hand, was to see commitment at its highest level. When we finally saw light at the end of a long dark tunnel, our trains no longer needed oars and we were back in business. I was a walking zombie at the end of those four days, but I was also ecstatic. Forty million gallons of water pumped out in four days—an amazing effort! And in less than a night we managed to build an entire new station. Emergencies seem to make people shine at the Authority, and shine they did. When I reflect on that time I have such a sense of pride in the "team." You see, during a crisis, everyone is focused on the goal-getting the service running. The commitment and energy gives all involved a remarkable sense of accomplishment.

LOSING A DRIVER

Another awful disaster happened shortly after I was named General Manager. I was walking through the kitchen in my shorts, as I caught a news flash on Channel 4 that reported a bus had just gone into the Charles River. I was the General Manager and yet I got this tragic information on the news! In the chaos of the moment the Dispatcher hadn't yet informed me.

I was dressed in seconds. I leaped into my car, my lights and siren on, and raced full out for the bridge where the news had reported the bus had last been seen. All the way there, I could envision that bus full of people, maybe 40 of them, a full load, and my head throbbed with a terrible foreboding. I figured they were all drowned. It was the dead of winter, close to zero, and although I had rushed out of my house without a coat and in sneakers. A thin sheen of sweat covered my forehead, indicating that my stress was at the highest level.

We spent nearly four hours retrieving the bus. When it was finally out of the water, divers went into the hatch to remove the individuals, and they discovered that except for the driver, slumped over his steering wheel dead, the bus was empty. At first I thought it must be a stolen bus because it wasn't scheduled to be on that road at that hour and I had no idea how it got there. We had floodlights everywhere, and when the divers pulled the driver out of the hatch, my knees went weak when the light reflected off of the patch on his sleeve, He was a T employee. I didn't know him. All I knew was, it was one of our own who had lost his life and there was no information as to why, and information is vital or tragedies remain unsolved. I had to send somebody to his house to tell his wife and children that he wasn't coming home for dinner any more and I was devastated for them. The press, as always, asked a million questions that you wanted to stuff back down their throats such as: *"How do you feel?"* What do you mean I thought to myself, *how do I feel? We lost a driver. "Was he drunk? Is the Authority at fault?"* On and on and on. Not only had we lost a human life, we had lost a fellow employee. I had grown up at the T and we were family. We wore the uniform proudly and we did the work. Having driven a bus myself, his death had an especially profound effect on me. It bothered me a lot; sleep didn't come easily for a long while. During my time as General Manager quite a few people died on the job, and when someone died, a piece of me died too. I don't mean to sound morbid, but as the leader you have to deal with the grief and, hardest of all, keep it inside, because you can't take it home with you any more than a cop can take home drug busts and murders. If you're married, you want to protect your spouse from some of the harsher realities of your job, and if you have children, you tend to become even more protective. Sometimes you have a conversation with your spouse, who needs to share what you're going through, but you try not to bring it home with you. You try to listen to what your family has to say and what's going on in their lives and to put the bad part of your personal tragic experiences to rest. In doing this, there is no avoiding the sleepless nights. I guess in hindsight keeping my sadness to myself in an effort to protect my family can be seen as a personal flaw and one I wished I had been more open with family about my feelings. I suppose that this is part of the "only child " syndrome. Pain makes you recoil.

VIEW FROM THE TOP

I believe the flood of '96 was my defining moment at the Authority. Six months later, Patrick Moynihan (not to be confused with the late U. S. Senator from New York) resigned as General Manager to become Secretary of Transportation. The board of directors had always recommended a nationwide search to fill the position, but not this time. The Authority had been through tumultuous changes and the feeling was that stability was needed at this point. The decision-making folks were convinced that I knew what I was talking about. Staying on top of Operations was my strong point, not politicking, and the powers-that-be liked that. I had paid my dues with more than 20 years of service. I cared about the people who worked at the MBTA and the people we worked for—the daily commuters. I had proven that I was willing to lay down my life to make the job of transportation work. The perception of me was that I would work a 25-hour day if I could somehow locate that extra hour—and they were right.

I would be the first African-American to head the authority, the expectations—and the questions—were huge. It was hard for me to believe at first that I was being considered for the top spot in the MBTA. Me? Bob Prince? The black guy who year's earlier drove a city bus and was happy doing it? I had to keep telling myself that this wasn't some impossible dream from which at any moment I would awake. I figured I was lucky, but I also figured I had earned my luck. Nobody gave me anything free along the way. My luck, if you want to call it that, had to be earned inch by inch. I believe in Affirmative Action, I believe it is an absolute necessity in our society, but in my case the only Affirmative Action that helped me was the affirmative attitude I brought to my work day by day. And it proved to be enough. I was never satisfied standing still. A lot of people, once they reach a certain level, find a comfort zone: this is it, I don't have to strive for anything more. If a bus driver for the Authority wants to be a bus driver and nothing else, I have the utmost respect for that. Drivers are the backbone of the T and they're in the public eye every moment of the working day. They're not likely to accept a promotion to an Inspector's (or as we call it, an Official's) job, as I did, because that would mean working nights or losing your "rating," and for many people working nights is psychologically a step in the wrong direction. Some folks don't want to have to supervise their friends, either, which is a totally understandable reaction. Early in my career I was called the Prince of Darkness, not for any demonic reason but because each time I got a promotion it seems that I was back on the night shift—and, of course, because my name happens to be

Prince. That was the downside of moving ahead: you lost some of the privileges you had worked so hard to accrue. Still, moving up the T ladder from bus driver to Night Supervisor held many delights. There wasn't a whole lot of training in those days. Basically, you were handed a set of keys and left pretty much alone to find your way.

The same could be said for becoming General Manager of the T. Again you're handed all of the keys and told, in effect that you're on your own—no road map, no guidelines, no blueprint—have a nice day. In July of 1997, when I was approached about the possibility of becoming General Manager, frankly I was flabbergasted. How could they put Bob Prince, a black man, in one of the key jobs in the entire state, I would be charged with running an enormous, complex business that employs more than 6,500 people and that directly affects practically every citizen in Boston and environs? How could that be? It was hard to get my mind around it. I have always been a pretty low profile kind of person and I didn't relish being the guy out front. I had never had a problem doing everything possible to make the boss look good, but now I would be the boss and would have to carry the banner. I would make the speeches, get my name in the newspapers and on TV, and I wasn't at all certain I was the person to do it.

I got called to the Boardroom and the members were staring me in the face. It was all I could do to keep the famous Prince cool. My mind was racing a million miles an hour because after a lot of hemming and hawing no one had come quite to the point. Finally, one of the members leaned toward me and asked me directly if I would consider becoming General Manager. I said that I was happy where I was but I was flattered by the offer. I didn't tell them that I was scared to death at the thought of having the entire T under me. I had plenty of belief in myself as a person and in my professional abilities, but did I have *that* level of belief?

Once the job was actually offered to me, the first phone call I made was to my cousin Walter Prince, who at one time had been General Council at the T and was now in private practice. I said, "Walter, do you think I'm the guy for the job? I need you to level with me on this. Do you think I have what it takes?" He said, "Are you excited about breaking in another General Manager? You've been there, done that. Maybe it's time to take the plunge. And besides, if not you, who, and if not now, when? These chances aren't handed to you every day."

We talked for more than an hour and then I went home and laid it all out for my wife and family, and with their blessing I decided to accept the position. I managed to convince myself that just maybe I *was* the guy for the job. I knew operations as well as or better than anybody. After all, I'd held most of the jobs at the T at one time or another. I knew from experience that there was no manual to show you how to run the organization. I'm sure the employees think the General Manager has a leadership concept firmly in place, but the truth is you have to feel your way along—kind of groping in the dark. You pick two or three goals you feel you can accomplish on your watch and work like hell on them before you get shot down. You also surround yourself with people you can trust. I found myself being approached by people who held the highest degrees from elite universities and who had fond hopes of becoming a part of my team. Prior to the announcement of my impending appointment as General Manager, most of those people were strangers to me. I decided to stick with those who had spent time with me in the trenches. Those were folks who would take a bullet for me—and me for them. They were also well educated; you could say they had post-graduate degrees in the intricacies of the T.

THE "SWEARING IN" THAT NEVER HAPPENED

Racism can take the oddest, most insidious forms, and it gave me a hard nudge the moment I became General Manager of the Authority. I had two bosses—the Secretary of Transportation and Chairman of the Board, who had succeeded the General Manager, and the Governor—I hold those two men accountable for an episode I'm about to reveal. What I am going to say disturbs me more than a little, but I feel compelled to set the record straight. I worked directly with the two prior General Managers, both of whom were sworn in by the Governor. In fact the ritual swearing in of new General Managers had a long history at the T. The ritual is purely symbolic and has no real relevance—or so I've been told. But is that actually true? Isn't it just as likely the case that embedded within the symbolic act is the reality of respect and honor for the recipient?

By tradition, the swearing in is administered at the time the new General Manager takes office. I was in office for six months and nothing happened; there was no mention of my being sworn in. Being an African-American, I was unique among all the General Managers in the 100-year history of the MBTA, because I was part of the history as the MBTA is America's First Subway System I was the MBTA's First African-American General Manager, a history maker. I am not too proud to say that I wanted the recognition that goes with the office. I particularly wanted it for my father. He was familiar enough with the workings of the Authority to know that I'd been ignored, and he was hurting inside. A former State Attorney General, who was a staunch Republican, promised me that he was personally going to see that the swearing in ceremony would happen because "it's the right thing to do." but it never happened in my four and a half years as GM.

I've thought a lot about the slight, and I've come to the conclusion that it wasn't an overt act of malice or racism. It was more a way of telling me that such rituals did not fit my special case. The transportation liaison for the Governor never met with me—never even called to congratulate me—which I thought was extremely odd. After a few months went by, I made an appointment to meet with the transportation liaison and also with the Governor's Chief of Staff. My action was a total breach of the chain of command, but I was determined that they realize I was my own person and that I was running the show. They said it was a shame I hadn't been officially sworn in at the time I became General Manager and claimed they appreciated my coming to see them to "air things out." During that meeting they were full of bonhomie and acted like I was a member in good standing of their exclusive club. The bottom line, though, was that they did nothing. I'm still waiting. I think it's going to be a mighty long wait.

But I had bigger issues than whether or not I was sworn in by the Governor. I was the new GM, the First black GM, and office politics reared its ugly head in all kinds of puzzling ways, both great and small.

THE OFFICE THAT BECAME A SHRINE

Two things happened as soon as the news got out that I'd been appointed General Manager. I think I'll start with intrigues in the corporate hallways of the T. I spent the first hour of my first day as General Manager staring at an office with bare walls, exposed cords, no bookshelves and minus a desk. This may seem small in the overall scheme of things, but in many ways my office problems were symbolic of the challenges ahead of me as a black CEO in a large corporation. This was not my first experience with the mysterious disappearance of such necessities. When I took over Operations, I left for an all-morning meeting, and when I returned, my office had been stripped bare except for the phone on the floor. I called Maryanne Walsh and told her I thought I'd been robbed. As it turned out, some mid-level executives from the other end of the corporate hall ("the boys," as we called them) had commandeered my furniture without informing Maryanne or me. And now as General Manager, it was, to quote Yogi Berra, déjà vu all over again. I was stripped clean again! Well, not entirely. "The boys" had left the carpet—partly, I suspect, because it was nailed down. In other words I made history on one end of the hall and was reminded of history on the other end, my historic accomplishment did not matter. We made out better than okay, though, as it happened. The only furniture available in the warehouse right then was elegant cherry with leather upholstery.

If you're wondering why the office of the top officer in the Authority was not ready for the new top officer, you have a right to wonder. I did my share of wondering myself that morning. The situation was definitely not normal, and I may have suffered a flash of paranoia that perhaps someone on the corporate corridor did not like me. Paranoia, I've been told, is nature's way of telling you that you've got enemies. The one piece of furniture that I was certain would never be removed was an antique fixture (railroad time clock) with no particular function that I could fathom. It had been drilled into the wall, and it had squatted there through the administrations of numerous General Managers. But on that first day, I saw that it was gone. All that remained were about six gaping holes in the wall. I never liked the damn fixture anyway, but I wondered why I was stripped even of that. Spoils of war.

Another curious incident occurred over the next few days that led to repercussions years later. I was given a Deputy, a decent enough fellow, easy to tolerate but not quite the triple A personality I would have chosen to juggle dozens of duties each day. He had been "thrust upon me," which made it a little harder to like him than would otherwise have been the case. Previous General Managers had been allowed to pick deputies of their choice. He worked with me for about a year and a half. Upon his departure, I met with the Secretary of Transportation and his Under Secretary, an African-American. I requested permission to move my Chief of Staff, Mikel Oglesby, also an African-American, into the now vacant office. I got the required permission, and that Friday Mikel moved into the office. By Friday evening, I received an irate phone call from the Secretary demanding to know who gave me permission to move Mikel into the office. It struck me as very odd indeed that the Secretary of Transportation, with his manifold duties, would somehow find the time to concern himself with the petty details of who sat where. But apparently he did have time, and he was adamant about Mikel not having that office. As embarrassing as it was, I told Mikel he would have to move back to his previous office and the office remained vacant.

Soon after that, I was given a new deputy and it turned out to be none other than the Secretary's former Under Secretary. There was one condition attached to adding him to my team, however. The Secretary made it clear that he was not to take over the office that the former deputy had occupied. By that point I was beginning to think that the office was being made into a shrine to honor my former deputy. I said to Maryanne, "Why don't we truck in some loam and plant flowers here?"

I decided that instead of letting the office remain vacant I would turn it into a conference room. Because he needed space, which was now not available, an office was built for him at a cost of $10,000. I'm no math major, but it seemed as though the Authority was wasting money to prove a point that at first eluded me, although even then I had a sneaking suspicion that the Secretary did not relish the idea of three blacks huddled together in the power corridor. My suspicion, unfortunately, became reality when he departed and Mike replaced him. Mike was a young smart Irish Catholic who had worked his way up through the ranks. I had considerable regard for Mike and still do (he became the next General Manager of the T.) Mike sat in what was the conference room for awhile until he approached me one day and asked if he could move into "The Shrine," as it had become known. He was fast outgrowing his space. I told him I had no problem with it but that he should first check with the Secretary's office. He was well liked down the hall, perhaps because he was white, he was Irish, he was Catholic (not bad things to be in the world of Boston). The very next day his secretary boxed his stuff up, and by quitting time "The Shrine" belonged to Mike. You can draw your own conclusions. I drew mine. But with all that I had on my plate I wasn't about to get caught up in the minutiae of race and office space. There were more important issues to handle. We had 28 unions, a 1 billion-dollar budget, and we provided service to 178 cities and towns and transported over 1 million passengers per day. Who sat in what office and why was not going to become any kind of priority for me. I suppose you could mark down the musical offices ongoing episode as just one more example of how hard it can be for an African American to truly make it in a white world. But there were more formidable obstacles to overcome. There was, for instance, a columnist, whose mission in life seemed to be to make my life miserable.

THE MEDIA BLITZ

From the day I was appointed General Manager, the media coverage I got from television and the newspapers hit me with hurricane force. The newspapers and TV detailed my years at the Authority and provided thumbnail sketches of this guy Bob Prince—a really huge guy, African-American, married with kids, not always an easy interview, a straight shooter, known to be a workaholic. He tells it like it is, but he's capable of putting his foot in his mouth. (The taste of one's shoes is not pleasant) In other words, I was no longer flying under the radar. I wasn't prepared for the media onslaught. Nor was I prepared as yet to dance with the press and make pretty for them. After a couple of major interviews, when I talked a little too much and was way too candid, I realized that I had a lot to learn. You have to master the art of measuring your words and trying to picture in your mind what those words will look like in cold print.

Some reporters were amused when I told them the story of the black cat. My appointment as General Manager coincided with the celebration of the 100th anniversary of the Authority. It took 100 years for the first black General Manager to arrive on the scene, but better late than never. I went on to explain (with a straight face) that there was a perfectly sound reason for my arrival at just this moment. It had a lot to do with the old folk tale that claims the first rider of the first MBTA trolley from Park Street to Boylston Street was a black cat (feline) named The Prince of The Subway. It seemed pretty clear to me that I had been reincarnated. As I said, most reporters were amused. One female African American reporter was not.

The columnist was a prolific writer with a large sharp ax to grind toward the Authority generally, especially when it came to issues of race. My name began appearing in her columns when I was head of Operations, neither I nor the GM escaped her wrath. She once referred to him as master of the slave ship. Her hyperbole aside, I didn't necessarily disagree with her about conditions at the T as I was one of the first people to admit that racism was alive and well in our Transit culture, a statement that did not win me any popularity contests among my T peers. When dealing with the Authority's 100-year-old culture, things like color and gender bias were not going to go away over night. We were just a microcosm of society as a whole. She wrote a series of ugly columns, and the tense relationship that grew between us had its origins in the first article she wrote on my watch. She hit hard on the glass ceiling issue and our unfair hiring practices, and she wondered why anyone thought these problems would suddenly disappear under my leadership. A lot of what she said was true; a lot, however, was distorted by her own set of biases.

I knew that she was taking information from a group of concerned minority employees and it was her mission to bring the T to its knees and make it accountable. Many of the issues she raised should have been properly handled through union representation, but the folks she talked to were trying to form a voice outside of that forum. I already had 28 unions, and I certainly did not need 29! Whether that was a right decision or not, it was my decision and I was willing to stick by it. I took the position that my energies were better served by creating training programs. I also adopted a policy of routing out unacceptable behavior and removing it from the workplace. The point is we did not, nor can society, cure racism; we went from overt to covert acts. We just made people smarter.

A controversial discharge came when an employee uttered the "N" word during the course of a radio conversation. This employee had been on the job for 22 years and was a year away from retirement. Like all of our personnel, he had been trained on zero tolerance. It was a tough situation for me. This individual and I had joined the T together and in many ways he was a good guy. I was aware that the NAACP would be all over me like a bad rash if I tolerated his behavior, and the Concerned Minority employees, a group of very vocal advocates for diversity, would also be all over me. With mixed feelings, I had to let him go. I couldn't get over the irony that the minority employees who came to his side to offer support during his trial and testified on his behalf, were the same people who were feeding the newspaper scuttlebutt on racist activities at the T. That bit of irony blew my mind.

One woman—who was black—testified that this employee was a fine worker and a solid citizen who deserved another chance. (Another bit of irony: she was co-chair of the Concerned Minority Employees.) She said that she had no problem with the word "nigger." I was both outraged and floored by her reaction. Had it gone the other way, had I let the man off with another stern warning, those same people would have taken me to task. That incident, in microcosm, was the story of my life at the T. You try as hard as you can to do the right thing and you get beaten up. You fight for diversity and both blacks and whites come down on you. The blacks say you haven't done enough and the whites say you're doing too much. Sometimes you feel caught in a no-win situation, but then I would comfort myself with the thought that if everyone is yelling for your scalp you must be doing something right.

The issues of race were systemic and my employees needed to be trained on what constituted acceptable behavior in the workplace and what did not. I was always up front about the institutional racism that existed (and still exists) at the T. The elephant was in the room and I was always willing to confront it. I made no attempt to gloss it over and say that everything would be just fine and we would all be singing Kumbaya and taking long walks on the beach together. That was not going to happen. Racism is like cancer. You can't treat it unless you know you've got it, and the only way to treat it is to bring it out in the open to cut it out. I spent a lot of time working with various groups, putting together educational programs, and making sure that T employees understood what type of behavior would not be tolerated. I couldn't legislate their beliefs but I could legislate their behavior in the workplace. My efforts to leach out bigotry were not going to happen overnight at the T—or anywhere else for that matter. Some folks thought that because I was black I could come up with an instant cure for all our problems. I found it interesting that my white counterparts were not charged with the same mission. I often had to remind people that I wasn't Martin Luther King, and that if I were to solve issues of racism during my watch, then I should be the next recipient of the Nobel Peace Prize.

I think that news reporter expected miracles from me because I was black. Nothing I did seemed to satisfy her. Having run up against some of the issues she raised in her columns that were on a very personal level, I wasn't unsympathetic to her point of view, but I also recognized that you had to work within the system to get it right and try to fix it. Being African-American myself, and being General Manager, it wasn't possible to focus all of my attention on one area. First of all, I would be shot down, and just as important, I had a bigger mission as the Authority's first General Manager of color. It was imperative that people understand that I was on the job for all the employees, not just a chosen few. I was also there for the customers and all of the taxpayers, not just those of a certain race.

This reporter clearly did not see it my way. She demanded action and she demanded it now. It didn't matter to her that my main mission was to do right for the State of Massachusetts. Her criticism of me was bold. She was very up front in saying that I was being manipulated by the higher ups in the state government. She characterized me as your basic "Uncle Tom." She wrote that I was part of the problem and not part of the solution.

When I got thoroughly fed up, I decided to invite her to lunch and thrash the issues out across a very small table. I figured it would be harder for her to write such scurrilous things about someone she had met and lunched with, someone who was willing to engage her point by point and one on one. It turned out to be a very pleasant lunch, and we were surprisingly open with each other. She asked me if I believed that racism could ever be cured in America, and my answer was absolutely, unequivocally not. You simply cannot get there from where we are today. Color separates us and culture separates us, and we try to deny the many meanings of those differences by driving them underground or pretending they don't exist. The best we can do, I told her, is educate each new generation, encourage mutual respect and punish those who persist in perpetuating evil.

She warmed to me and we certainly stood on common ground. She continued to write about me and the Authority, and by no means in ringing tones of endorsement, but from then on she would call and give me a heads up when she planned to publish a piece. The pieces that she wrote continued not to please me, but at least she was willing to discuss them with me later and we had some soul searching dialogues. She was in the business of selling newspapers and I was in the business of transportation, and even after our thaw she never stopped trying to make my life a little more difficult.

This may sound strange, but I felt sorry for her when, sometime later, she was fired from the newspaper for a story she wrote in which she did some unforgivable embellishing. It was a story, by the way, which had nothing to do with the Authority. A reporter from another paper called me wanting a statement about her being fired. I told her that I gained no joy from her job loss. I thought that everybody lost. She was a very good writer with a real passion and with strong ideals. She may not have met the journalistic standards of the newspaper, at least on that one story, but I hoped that before long she would find a place where her voice could be heard. I have no idea what became of her.

THE CURIOUS CASE OF THE COMPANY CAR

She was not the only reporter who took potshots at me. There was also another reporter, and I'll get to him in a moment. As I've already said, people of color expected miracles of me when I became General Manager. It was as though Martin Luther King had just stepped up to the plate to hit a homerun for the entire black race. But because I was a Prince, not a King, I was instantly flawed, insincere, found wanting. For white people my arrival on the scene was sort of like, "Oh Jesus, what do we have here? What have we let ourselves in for?" Many of them had nightmares of reverse discrimination. I felt that I had the support of those who knew me well, but that was a small group in the beginning. The press had taken potshots at me even before I became General Manager. I have always attracted press coverage, and the irony is that I hated every minute of it. I've never made a secret of my distrust and sometimes loathing for the press. Reporters are a necessary evil in a free society, but that doesn't mean I have to like them or consider them anything less than a pain in the backside, and often a real impediment to getting things done. One issue certain reporters kept raising about me was the company cars I drove. They also wrote about my driver, Leo Rogers, a white man and a friend—a guy I would trust with my life.

Now we are about to delve into a piece of racial geometry. If you're a white GM, finding a driver is a snap. Everybody will line up to drive for you; there is no stigma attached. But if you're a black GM looking for a driver, you find that there isn't a long waiting list of those who want to be driving Mr. Daisy. This is one more example—albeit a small one—of how ticklish it is to be the black CEO of a large organization. If I hired a white chauffeur (which I did), many folks would consider me an uppity black man (and some did). A woman chauffeur would be out of the question because the media would have me sleeping with her. (Black men and their sexual prowess—another white nightmare.) I could hire a black driver but that would look like racial favoritism. I could always drive myself, but the GM was required to have a driver. So I had Leo.

Leo Rogers and I were bonded for many reasons, and one had to do with the famous case of the Naked Lady on the Subway—by now a piece of T lore. Years before I became GM the two of us were inspectors working out of the Orient Heights station on the Blue Line. A call came in that a woman at Beachmont Station had passed out on the train. I said that I would call an ambulance and meet the train when it reached Orient Heights. Seconds later, the phone rang again and the dispatcher said, "Hey, she's not passed out. She's taking off her clothes." I told him to isolate the car. When the train pulled into Orient Heights, Leo and I boarded the third car and sure enough a woman was standing with her back to me naked as a jaybird. I said, "Madam, whatever your issues are, I'm sure we can resolve them. Let's gather up your things, get off the train and we can talk." "Don't touch me," she replied, her back still to me. I said, "I have no thoughts about putting my hands on you." She then turned around and looked at me. "Oh, you're black," she said. "Uh-huh," I answered. "Now let's go." She suddenly dropped to her knees, grabbed me around the ankles and started kissing my boots. By now the platform was full of people looking on and I could just visualize the newspaper's take on the event the next morning.

Leo was standing in the doorway of the car beet red and trying to control his laughter. I wasn't sure whether I should manhandle the woman off the train or try to sweet talk her off, or what to do. After a struggle I finally talked her into dressing herself. She was a young Greek woman, in her early 20s, and betrothed to an older gentleman. When he arrived at the station to pick her up, she once again dropped to her knees and began kissing his shoes. I never did understand what the kissing of the feet thing signified, but I can tell you that the story made a circuit of the T faster than you can blink an eye.

When I became General Manager of the Authority I needed somebody I could trust, and Leo was my obvious choice. There's no question that he loved the job. It put him in the GM's office in a suit and tie, and wherever I went he went. He made my appointments for me, he helped me to avoid people who were out to cause trouble or to waste my time, and secrets were locked inside of him like a vault.

But I must return to the curious case of the company car—the newspaper's obsession. The car I inherited when I took over was a Blazer, but I'm a big guy and the Blazer is a tight fit at best, so I opted for an Expedition. I bought it right off the rack with no special features, but the paper wrote about the car as though I'd just sprung for a custom made Rolls Royce. It didn't matter that the Mayor had an Expedition; the Secretary of Transportation had one; the Chairperson of the Mass Turnpike had one; and the head of Massport had one. And their Expeditions were all decked out with every possible feature; including leather seats (my car had cloth seats). But why did Prince feel that he rated an Expedition? One day I ran into the reporter I mentioned earlier (he had sniped at me about my outrageous sense of entitlement), and I said, "Let me give you a ride in my car because you seem so fixated on it. When he got in he said, "There's no leather seats in here." I said, "That's right. No leather seats, no CD. I only have what it came with. It came with air conditioning." After that, the newspaper began to leave me alone. I'm pretty sure that if a large white general manager had bought himself an Expedition the newspaper wouldn't have thought it worth reporting on. But the black CEO is always news, and the newspapers, after all, is in the business of selling papers.

I also got plenty of exposure on television, both good and bad. Because race and controversy draw viewers in, I was asked to participate on a lot of shows dealing with race that tackled the institutional racism that was still very much in evidence at the T. We were making headway, a little at a time, and diversity in employment was up from 27.6 percent to 30.4 percent among minorities and from 20.9 percent to 22.8 percent among women—better figures than any other governmental agency in the Commonwealth. It's important to note that in 1975 the year prior to my joining the MBTA, the work force diversity numbers were: 94% white males 2.8% people of color and 2.7% females. In my 20 year tenure prior to becoming GM there was lots of change, and with change came lots of tension. People, and particularly minorities, felt that we were doing a poor job even so. That really troubled me. An acquaintance of mine, a brilliant woman, spoke for many, I think, when she stated that I had sold out as GM. She told me that straight to my face and I admired her candor, but she was wrong. I never sold out. I fought every day to make the Authority a better workplace, a more level playing field, which was better attuned to the needs of the traveling public. But people sometimes forget that the T is a huge place, a city within a city. It has its own medical complex, it has its own lawyers, it has its own carpenters and black-smiths and mental health workers. And it's all about the business of running buses, trains, trolleys and boats and getting people to and from work safely and on time. I worked hard from the minute I became General Manager never to lose touch with the T on any level. Sometimes I would get up at dawn to make the shifts and find out what folks were thinking and feeling. Most people on the job trusted me because I came from where they came from. My main virtue as a boss was that I was not seen as just another bureaucrat or hack politician trying to worm into their good graces. They viewed me as a bus driver who just happened to be a rung higher up on the bureaucratic ladder, which was exactly the way I wanted it to be. In the Navy there is an old saying: loyalty up and loyalty down. I believe in that with all my heart. I would not expect anything from anyone that I would not give back in equal measure. To me, that is the human way and the democratic way.

When it was time for me to move on, I recommended my former Deputy for the job as General Manager. He was smart and solid, and best of all as a White Irish Bostonian he represented a comfort level for the powers-that-be. He would run the Authority without a breath of controversy. He was not about to make news because he avoids news and controversy like the plague. He doesn't sell papers, and I was selling papers left and right during my nearly five tumultuous years as GM. Hell, I should have bought stock in the newspaper I helped sell.

THE GREAT TOM KATS CONTROVERSY

It seems that wherever I turned, controversy found me as unerringly as a bee finds honey. Witness the firestorm over a lame movie called *Tom Kats*. The hullabaloo put me in a very difficult position ethically and even politically. The thought that stopping an ad that was about to go up on the transit system would create an outcry never occurred to me, and maybe that was naïve on my part. I didn't reckon with the newspapers invoking the First Amendment and calling me anti-democratic. I believe in the U.S. Constitution; to me it is one of the most precious documents ever conceived, but like all written records of the greatest importance, and I include the Bible in this, it is subject to interpretation. My decision to keep the lamentably stupid movie *Tom Kats* off the transit radar screen put me in a very awkward position.

The Authority's marketing department is responsible for ads that are placed on the Authority's buses, trolleys, trains and stations. Every once in a while during my watch, an ad would come along that struck me as inappropriate. The Authority carries thousands of children to their destination each day, and as General Manager I felt responsible for what they were exposed to. The first time I evoked my veto privilege was over an ad for a move comedy called *Baseketballs*, which pictured a man holding two large balls in his crotch area. My decision to can it generated some press, but we stood firm and the ad did not go up.

The second use of my executive privilege didn't go over so well and proved to be a very large headache. The ad for a movie called *Tom Kats* showed a scantily clad woman wearing a boa constrictor with the heads of several men gathered at her crotch area. The text implied that the last man standing would get the "Kitty." The boa was also sexually suggestive in its placement. When I said no to *Tom Kats* all hell broke loose. My decision drew national attention, and there were those who said I was un-American and against free speech.

In all probability, refusing to let the ad run in the system actually contributed to what success the movie had, which was far from my intention. The basis for the decision was to shield our riders—young children in particular—from indecent material. Transit riders are a captive audience; you put something in front of them and they are bound to stare at it and read it. They really have no other choice. I believed—and I still believe—that the Authority had an obligation not to subject them to questionable material. It seemed that the lion's share of people across the country agreed with me because we were flooded with letters, most of which were positive.

I suppose a case can be made that I rattled the chains of the American Civil Liberties Union (ACLU) in my own small way, and maybe I did. But the great thing about a democracy like ours is its flexibility. Most laws do not deal with rigid definitions of right and wrong in areas of free speech. There is always room for the gray shadings where some of the greatest struggles about ethics and morality are fought and resolved. In my judgment, the ACLU was no more wrong in questioning my motives and actions than I was in following my own moral compass.

Baseketballs and *Tom Kats* are indeed very small deals in the grand scheme of things, and I'm aware that there are those who considered me no better than a book burner, but I'm proud of the position I took. Put me back there and I would gladly make the same decision.

PROMISES MADE, PROMISES KEPT

I was excited about having the opportunity to run the Authority along some brand new pathways—excited, scared and incredulous, all at the same time. I knew that I wanted to leave my mark on the office. Jack Killgoar had taught me two important things, among many others. First, I should never believe my own press clippings because then I'd begin to take myself way too seriously. And second, I should make sure that any plan I embarked on would have at least a ten-year shelf life. In other words, whatever I set out to do should not be done for the flash or the buzz. It should be a lasting contribution. I planned to make changes in the service and changes in the workforce.

As I said earlier, you go into the top job with two or three tasks you hope to complete on your watch. One of my major goals was to finish the Orange Line. (The Orange Line was once an old elevated system that ran through the main street of an urban center; it was noisy and bleak, decreasing property values in the area.) The Orange Line southwest corridor was new and had been signalized only up to the State Street portion. I had to see that the work got completed, because in its unfinished state it was wreaking havoc with the timing of trains on the other lines. Another goal was to fix the four Dorchester stations. They were in very diverse neighborhoods that were going to fall down if they weren't repaired fast. Third, the Charles Street Station, where Mass General Hospital is located, was not accessible to the disabled community, and I was prepared to fight like a tiger to make it so. My fourth goal was to make the Silver Line bus rapid transit system a state-of-the-art means of commuting. This line would replace a portion of the aforementioned Orange Line rapid transit system, known as the El, which had been demolished.

The Silver Line was a make or break proposition for me, and it's no exaggeration to say it damn near broke me. The Silver Line runs through Roxbury, in the heart of the black community where I still make my home, and the service was desperately needed. One thing that differentiates buses from trains (and the Silver Line is a bus line) is that trains tend to run on time, whereas buses are subject to weather, traffic conditions and various other hazards. But as a bus driver, I had rarely been late to pick up passengers and I was going to make it plain to the drivers that they had an obligation to be on time—only legitimate excuses accepted. A GPS system was installed on the buses, which allowed the control center to give real time information on when the next bus would arrive; this information was then relayed to the kiosks where commuters were waiting, thus solving the major problem of uncertainty. If you're standing on the street in the middle of a snowstorm, it's important to know when the next bus is coming. If you're confident that it will arrive in three minutes, or five, or seven, you know whether you have time to duck into the 7-11 for a container of coffee. The success or failure of the Authority rests on those kinds of specific commitments to the traveling citizen: they are the heart and soul of our job. But as it turned out, I got no end of grief for the Silver Line. I was accused of providing the black community with substandard service, and many blacks were up in arms. They demanded light rail or trolley service on guided rail. Other communities had light rail—why couldn't they have it too? Was this just one more example of discrimination—of giving black folk less than the best? They believe to this day that rail gives a sense of permanence and I countered by saying that cleanliness, safety and on-time performance are what count. If I can give you all of those, I argued, it doesn't matter whether it's on a rail or rubber tire. This argument was a sign of things to come: many blacks were convinced that their black General Manager, instead of acting like the Martin Luther King of the transportation system, the man who would make all things right, had sold out to the power elite.

The situation on the Red Line in Dorchester was a happier one because the community wanted improvement to happen. The stations were old and needed to be repaired or rebuilt. Although it was good that the community was positive and involved, there can also be a downside to over enthusiasm; sometimes process kills progress when too many people insist on becoming involved. You try to explain you're working under time pressure and that the goal is not to build the Taj Mahal but something that blends with the architecture of the neighborhood while keeping costs within the budget. That's a tough message to get across when people are hell bent on building something better than whatever the next community has. It's a case of keeping up with the Joneses on a massive scale.

How the money was raised to improve the Red Line is an insight into how the Authority works. I was called to the office of the Speaker of the House of Representatives, who happened to also represent that area of Dorchester. It was just the two of us talking; there were no entourages. I outlined the massive reconstruction plan and when I was finished he asked me if I had the money in the budget for these station upgrades. "Absolutely not," I said. "Well then," he said, "we have to find a creative way to find the money. I'll call you when I get it done, Bob." Saturday morning as I was on my way to the wedding of a woman who worked at the Authority, The Speaker called to say he had the money lined up. As I remember it was $65 million. "Make no mistake," he said, "the money is for those stations. It's not to spread around." "I understand," I said. I hung up riding on a high. Dorchester, the "melting pot" of Boston, deserved a happy ending. The stations we were about to improve ran through every ethnic walk of life.

A week later, I had my regular weekly meeting with my boss, the Secretary of Transportation for the State of Massachusetts. With a satisfied smile, he told me that we had the money for the Red Line stations. He had no inkling that I already knew, and it was also clear that he had only the haziest idea of the Speaker's role in raising the cash. The Secretary was all bubbly and effusive as though he had just pulled off the neatest trick of the year, and that was okay by me. I wanted no credit. Let him use this bonanza for his own political gain. The Secretary of Transportation was a political appointment and on his playing field it was all about politics. Under the Secretary's jurisdiction were Massachusetts Highway, the MBTA and Massachusetts Aeronautics, and each branch had its own separate funding. The hard fact was that the Secretary and the Highway Commissioner had sat on their hands when it came to finding money for the project; their constant refrain was that they didn't have the money and without the money the work couldn't be done. I had argued with them until I was blue in the face that I had committed myself to the community. I said we were going to fix those stations and I was not going to come out of this a liar. Nobody believed me, and yet it got done, and exactly how it was done nobody ever knew. That's a small but telling insight into the separation of powers.

I should add here that I had my issues with the Secretary of Transportation from day one. I was an "operations guy" and always had been, and he was a political appointee. When I told him how gung-ho I was to build the Silver Line, his response was, "Those people" don't want it. You should leave well enough alone and concentrate your efforts elsewhere. "Define 'those people'," I said. After all, I was one of "those people" myself. The communities I was dealing with in the early stages of my tenure were predominantly African-American, so I could only assume that he was implying that the black people in the community were opposed to the Silver Line. And unfortunately he was more right than not. Many of them, as I've mentioned, felt cheated by not getting rail service. But I knew that he was right for the wrong reasons. In his mindset, black communities did not deserve the same priority as the more affluent ones.

The Silver Line was going to get done, I vowed, because my reputation was out there on the line, and I wasn't about to see a lot of hard work and planning just blown off. It had been years since the Orange Line had been removed from this area, and I wasn't going to wait for a handful of new General Managers to decide to complete the job. Not having the support of the Secretary of Transportation was one thing, but being dissed by the black community was what really gave me an ache in the gut. They were willing to hurt themselves out of a sense of misplaced pride: they wanted light rail and nothing else would do, and how come their black brother wouldn't fight to give it to them? The situation became so heated that when the work actually got underway the black legislative caucus boycotted the groundbreaking, which was scheduled while I was on a business trip in California. I flew in on the red eye, and had to share the dais with the Highway Commissioner. When a photographer set up a shot with the shovels, I had to share a shovel with the Highway Commissioner because there wasn't a shovel for me. There were at least a dozen people in the picture whom I didn't even recognize. But was I irritated by this obvious attempt for a lot of folks to make political hay? I can honestly say that I couldn't have cared less. It wasn't about claiming who did what and who should get the credit. The only question of any importance was whether or not the Silver Line was going to be built—and, yes, it *was* going to be built. That was all that mattered.

The other goal I hoped to accomplish on my watch was to train all T employees in the delicate nuances surrounding the issue of diversity. I hoped to create an environment for all of our workers free of hostility and to create an atmosphere where they could do their best work. I worked to improve hiring practices for women and minorities. I knew this was going to be an uphill climb, but I was more than ready for the scramble up the steep mountainside.

HOW THE POWER WORKS

The Secretary of Transportation during my time as General Manager was a highly political individual, but I certainly was not chosen for political reasons. I believe his main concern was to install an operations man whose primary function was to run the transportation system. The politics would take care of itself. I was no power broker. I was no political magician. I wasn't someone who had a vested interest in making sure that my brothers and sisters of color got cushy sinecures. I was however able to give many talented people of color opportunities at the MBTA. The Secretary and the Governor knew that I was pretty even handed in that area. But as it turned out, there was no avoiding politics; it was in the air I breathed.

The T is a unique place because you can become a big time power broker if that's your fancy. The T has the money, it has the power, and it has the jobs. If you have the controlling hand on all those levers you are a major player in the State of Massachusetts. When I first entered the management side of the business, hiring for entry level positions was done basically in two ways. The bulk of the hiring was done through a lottery system, which couldn't be tampered with and which gave equal access to all. The second way was political (mainly in the management and upper management areas, particularly when the Republicans held office, but also on the lower rungs). Anyone who says otherwise is lying. You got the job through political contacts. Back then I used to keep three lists: the Democratic list, the Republican list, and the this-person-is-deserving-of-a-job list. As much as I hated the political aspects of management, there was no way to stay totally out of that game. By judicial hiring practices, I was able to survive both political parties, regardless of which one was in power. But it was the third list that gave a measure of legitimacy to our hiring practices. If we were hiring nine people, I made sure there were some non-political hires on that list. Once I became General Manager, I was the gatekeeper. I made the recommendations, and I controlled the lists. But keeping the third list viable wasn't easy. Slowly, through a push for greater diversity in hiring, the purely political hiring began to decline.

But when I first took over, political hiring was a hot button issue. It was a culture that could not be changed overnight. This was the way it worked: The Governor's office would call down and say that certain people had to be hired; they were called "must-do" people. The Governor, after all, had his constituency, and he wanted to take care of key people who had worked on his campaign. And it's worth mentioning that jobs at the T were very good indeed and paid handsome salaries.

The Democrats were prone to push for the more blue-collar positions—running a train, for instance—jobs that offered longevity. Those were union positions, and the Democrats held sway over the unions. The Republicans, on the other hand, pushed for positions as Supervisors, Directors of various divisions, or Managers. There are only so many of those jobs available, so a good deal of creativity was needed to satisfy the Republicans.

While I worked hard to balance all of these political complexities, we were making progress on the diversity front, and yet, ironically, we were getting beat up by the press on that very issue. A lot of big businesses in Massachusetts didn't have any problems with diversity because they didn't have any diversity to begin with. If you have only a handful of minority employees, they aren't going to be ranting and raving about how the old boy network is keeping you down. But when you have a large, diverse workforce with a voice of its own, that voice will speak out loud and clear and articulate its needs. We were being attacked for a program that was working better than most, which led me to the inevitable conclusion that if you do well on diversity, you're going to run into diversity problems. The more you do, the more is expected of you. Take, for example, our push for diversity among bus drivers. We fought to have the people who operated the equipment fit into the neighborhoods they were serving. A black driver in a black neighborhood made the best kind of common sense. At the same time, women began to fill the system in key positions, such as Head of Operations and Commuter Rail, Head of Revenue and Head of Safety. It seems that if you do poorly on diversity, you don't create a voice of opposition to leadership, and you don't get beat up. Here we were with the best diversity numbers in the state and yet the newspapers were killing us on the issue—plus we were being criticized by many of the folks within our own unions. Still, with all the problems we faced, I wouldn't have had it any other way. As head of the Authority I got to see the big picture, which told me loud and clear that we were making progress. But I came to realize all too soon that I couldn't fix all the problems. There is no James Jones formula where followers drink the Kool-Aid and suddenly become righteous. It just was not going to happen except in small increments. All I could do was the best I was capable of with the cards I was dealt.

THE FTA-AMTRAK BLUES

Diversity issues and the political agonies of dealing with the Secretary of Transportation were far from the only problems that kept me awake at night. There was also the peculiar behavior of an oversight agency about our relationship with Amtrak. Let me be quick to say that the agency was at that time our industry's greatest benefactor. They always supported us as we always supported them. We were family. Which makes it all the more difficult to understand the agency's actions in Boston in 1999. That year, at their urging, we opened up the bidding process for our passenger rail contracts. Shortly after that, a firestorm of controversy erupted. Until then, Amtrak had been our sole contract provider, and the only future provider capable of bidding on the total MBTA package. To generate competing bids, at the behest of the agency and with their full compliance and knowledge, we unbundled the contract package. ["In order to..." is really the same as "To..." and the single word is more efficient.] We then asked for separate bids for portions of the contract, such as service operations and right-of-way. Bids came back with unbelievable savings. No one could have guessed there would be a $116 million difference between Amtrak's contract and what we were offered by competitive bidders. It was a no-brainer for us. Management would have been foolish and irresponsible not to move forward with the new bids. But when we went ahead to cement the new arrangement, hardball politics hit us like a hurricane.

Everyone involved in the negotiations knew that Amtrak would not go down without a fight. Local forces were unleashed first. The local legislature hammered us by suggesting massive job loss and other crimes against constituents. Then came the national forces—politicians and labor leaders—amassing their collective strength against the T. We suddenly found ourselves standing alone. We were looking at a losing chess position—damned if we made the deal, damned if we didn't. The local press joined the feeding frenzy, devouring us in large chunks, and the rest is history.

The long and the short of it is that we were forced to back down. We were made to look both venal and foolish, when, in fact, we were the only ones in all that mess trying to make a change for more efficient and cheaper passenger service—which begs the question. Where was the oversight group when things got hot? In the rough and tumble world of national politics, no matter where you stood on the Amtrak issue, no one could blame Amtrak or its political supporters for trying to protect their northeastern turf. Nor could anyone blame labor for protecting its workers. Those groups were upfront about their intentions. But what were the intentions of the agency in urging us to open up the bidding process? Where were they when we needed them? After all, they had pressed for the open bidding concept and now they were nowhere to be found.

All of us honchos at the Authority took more bullets over this issue than Clint Eastwood's bus in *The Gauntlet*. Some might argue that many of those shots were taken for the agency, which in the end thanked us by holding up federal funds for vital transit projects in Boston. If the oversight officials had no intention of backing the T when the going got rough, why did they encourage us to unbundle the contract in the first place? That seems to be the million dollar unanswered question. They must have known that the Amtrak contract, if lost in Boston, would have important ramifications nationwide. Other transit organizations around the country surely would follow suit and pursue cost-saving contracts with other providers. The agency surely was aware that Amtrak would pull out all stops to crush our plans. At the very least, while they were encouraging us to unbundle and bid out, they could have briefed us on the national consequences of these actions. Then we could have made an informed choice whether to pursue such folly without guaranteed assurances of the agency's backing.

Even though the oversight officials cannot be blamed entirely for the contract debacle, their run-for-cover posture, their deafening silence and their no-show support for the Authority left a bitter taste, especially because we had come to expect so much more from our transportation leaders in Washington. I would like to be able to state the agency's viewpoint, should they ever offer one, for the curious position they took. It was a position that nearly created major disaster for the T, and yet they never offered so much as an explanation for their behavior or an apology. I'm still left wondering what possible motivation they had for putting us in such a difficult position and then abandoning us to face the consequences.

It seems likely that I will never know.

THE MILLENNIUM

Preparations for the millennium devoured large chucks of my time and energy over a period of eighteen months. In our fast-moving world it's easy to forget that as the clock ticked down to January 1, 2000 all kinds of horrific catastrophes were predicted, from bombings to worldwide computer crashes. We needed to fine-tune all of our policies and procedures in case any of the countless dire scenarios being broadcast daily in the newspapers and on TV actually came to pass. We worked with other agencies on tabletop drills. Our goal was to figure out how we could contain the area and continue to run service.

A tragedy that had taken place a few years earlier gave us clues on what we might be facing on a much larger scale. While I still worked in Operations, a Commuter Rail standing locomotive was hit head on by another train that was traveling at a speed of 100 miles an hour. It was the worst crash the Authority had ever suffered. The standing train was telescoped and punched up through the street. Jack Killgoar and I got to the site about twenty minutes after the accident and a grisly scene confronted us: amidst a constant chorus of groans and moaning, bodies were strewn about; cars were on fire and tipped on their sides. Being a natural-born leader, Jack instantly took the reins. He quickly organized the evacuation of victims from the crumpled cars and enforced strict crowd control. He sent me to North Station to start turning trains to get the Orange Line running at a higher capacity. Accommodating customers, even in the midst of human tragedy, was his first priority. He knew that emergency personnel were en route to the scene, and he put me to better use. So in a three-piece suit I rushed down to North Station and started throwing switches used to turn the trains so that we could better use our service.

We used our experiences from that crash to practice for potential millennium disasters and to map out contingency plans. We established points of control internally, working closely with Boston Fire, Boston Police and the EMTs. We trained all employees on how to respond to possible chaos. These were stressful exercises for me as General Manager, because if the system went down and couldn't quickly be up and running you could rest assured that as the agency leader I would take the lion's share of the blame. It came as no surprise to my family that I worked through the night of December 31, 1999, well into the morning of the first day of the next 1,000 years. In fact, during my stint as GM I never had a New Year's Eve off. I figured if my fare collectors and drivers and fellow officers had to be out there on the line, I should be there too. I wasn't rushing off to any parties. It was all about making sure that we kept the service running and kept the celebrants using our service safely. [???]

As it happened, January 1st, 2000 came and passed without incident. But eighteen months and eleven days later on September 11, 2001, we were indeed as shocked as was the rest of America.

9/11

All of the things we had trained for during the millennium period helped us through one of the darkest pages in our history. Every minute of that beautiful sunny late fall day in September still lives in my memory with perfect clarity. I have a TV in my office and I watched the second plane crash into the South Tower of the World Trade Center. I sat transfixed staring at the rings of fire that enveloped the two towers. There was no time to watch television as I was on the phone with the Chief of Police when the South Tower came down. The Secretary of Transportation and I were finalizing plans to evacuate Boston when the North Tower came down. My TV was still on but I was not aware that the towers had fallen until someone rushed into my office and informed me.

Although I was just a couple of months from retiring when the terrorists hit New York and the Pentagon in Washington D. C, I was still very much on the job. I can say without fear of contradiction that the major transportation agencies across this country kept us from going into a major state of gridlock. The New York Transit Authority, and Path—despite what the 9/11 Commission says—performed valiantly in getting people out of the core areas. While the firemen, the police, the steelworkers and volunteers from other cities were lauded for their bravery—as indeed they deserved to be—the New York Transit Authority was never given much national coverage. Transportation authorities are taken for granted when the trains and buses run on time, but are severely criticized when things go wrong. That is simply the reality of the job.

As General Manager of the Authority, it was my responsibility to plan for the worst, but when a 9/11 happens or a major catastrophe like the saran gas release in Japan, all you can do is try to minimize the number of people who could potentially die. The lesson of 9/11 is that we are going to have to rethink our responses to attack. Transit people are like fire horses; they hear the bell and then run to the fire. But given the type of terrorism we're now dealing with you cannot simply run to the fire and put it out. You may not even know what kind of fire you're running to.

Many of the contingency plans we had trained for during the millennium period quickly fell into place. I was taken by police car, along with the Secretary of Transportation, in a convoy following the Governor to the "Bunker"(Massachusetts Emergency Management center) out in Framingham. On our way there, one of the state cruisers was hit by another car and the Director of Public Safety ended up riding in our car. It's amazing what goes through your mind when traveling at high speeds with the Chief of Police driving, lights and sirens blaring. I was saying to myself," please, God, make these tires hold up, for I have a month left to retire." When we got to the bunker, we were joined by top officials of the Army, the Navy, the Marine Corps, the Air Force, the State Police, the National Guard and Massport. We all briefed the Governor on our respective emergency plans. We were running watch trains staffed with police officers and we had already purchased bombproof barrels. We were testing a device that could detect any type of gas released in the system. My mind was going a million miles a minute. This was no longer an exercise. This was the real thing. I would like to be more specific as to systems the Authority put into place on that terrible day and be precise about how they were intended to work, but the information was proprietary then and remains so to this day. My lips are sealed.

I can honestly say it was the longest day of my life. It was surreal. I was about to retire and hand over the reins to Mike Mulhern. But there in the bunker, in the midst of fear and uncertainty, I was still in command. After the twin towers, the Pentagon was hit, and on all of our minds was a single thought: was Boston on the terrorists' list? If our system went down, I would be held accountable recognizing that the media would eat me for lunch, but it didn't happen that way. Our system kept running. In the weeks that followed, I watched with sinking heart the ordeal of the head of Massport and the person in charge of Logan Airport. She was now swinging in the breeze all by herself, taking the heat for something over which she'd had no control. If the terrorists had used one of the Authority's trains instead of deciding to fly out of Logan, I would have been the one out there swinging in the breeze. Carrying the burden of responsibility on your shoulders with no one to share the weight amounts to stress squared, and I thought the treatment of the Massport head was outrageous and unfair. It seems as though we had to have victims to answer for the victims who had perished at the World Trade Center, on the planes and at the Pentagon. The only thing people could focus on was that planes manned with terrorists had flown out of her area of responsibility. Case closed.

As for me, I retired unscathed. When I thought back on that terrible period I realized that my time at the Authority in a management capacity had been fraught with stress, which is one of the byproducts of being in a leadership role. Major catastrophes could occur at any time. I was head of Operations during the Oklahoma bombings, and I remember receiving a phone call stating that there was a specific threat on my property. I took a chance and shut the system down. It never ceases to amaze me how people will second-guess you *after* you make a decision. Luckily, I was right that time. During 9/11 I was once again faced with a fateful choice: keep the system running or shut it down. We were equipped to quit the entire system in ten minutes, and the decision was in my hands. I don't mind admitting that I was deathly afraid of making the wrong choice. I finally decided that we should evacuate the downtown Boston area. I feel that I made the right call, but when nothing happens, the Monday morning quarterbacks come crawling out of the woodwork calling for your head on a platter. But if something had gone very wrong and I had not ordered an evacuation, imagine the even greater beating I would have taken. I was the one who had to step up to the plate at that crucial moment on that sunny Tuesday morning of such a startling tragedy and I did what was expected of the leader, I made the decision. I've worked out a theory about hard choices. It goes like this: "I'll never chastise you for making a decision even if it's the wrong one. But I will chastise you for not making a decision at all."

If we learned anything of value from 9/11 it should have been that we, too, are vulnerable. Have we learned that lesson? I'm not sure that we have. Geography no longer safely separates us from those who wish to do us harm. Because we can get to anyplace in the world today in a nanosecond, others can reach us just as quickly. What makes us impervious to acts of terrorism? Nothing, is the answer. More than ever, we have to join the rest of the human race instead of soaring above others with our vaunted air power. We must avoid drawing into ourselves and cutting ourselves off from the needs and concerns of other countries. My secretary, Caroline, was born and brought up in Ireland. She said to me after 9/11, "Now you can see what I've lived with all my life. Buses being blown up, people being shot at all the time. Blood in the streets. It was just a way of life." I suspect that we do believe that something like 9/11 will happen again, and that we're doing everything possible to avoid it. I truly believe this is the best country in the world, offering the most promise for individual freedom, but it's time to wake up and smell the coffee. Perhaps as a black man in America I've smelled it longer than most. Recently I watched some talking heads on television, and they were discussing our national state of mental health. They mentioned the red and orange and yellow alerts, and I got the impression listening to them that another major terrorist attack was just around the corner, which would cause widespread panic. The stock market would collapse and everything else would fold up like cheap lawn furniture because we're not used to handling truly life-and-death issues in America. We talk tough, but how tough are we really? We've been living fat, dumb, happy lives for a long, long time. I think it's high time we join the rest of the human race and give up the idea of being the one imperial power on earth. It never lasted for other imperial powers, and it won't last for us either.

When those planes hit the twin towers, the very heart of this country's financial nexus, changed my way of thinking in many ways. Terrorists don't have to play fair, they don't have to abide by the Geneva Convention. They fight wars their way, and they fight us because they hate us. Maybe we shouldn't even call them terrorists, because they're really more than that. They are religious zealots who hate us for our Christian religion and for our invasions of other lands and for our wealth and our arrogance. Think of them that way and they look even more dangerous. These zealots are aware that what's most vulnerable is our mass transit systems—our bridges and subways, seaports and major highways. Do you want to shut down New York City? Hit the subway system. Do you want to shut down Boston? Hit the subway system. Every major urban city—Atlanta, Washington D.C., Chicago, San Francisco—is a transportation accident waiting to happen. You can put safeguards in place, but there's only so much you can do in this new kind of war, which is almost impossible to know how to fight. We don't check the airlines thoroughly, even now. You can ride on the AmTrak carrying a huge piece of luggage no one bothers to check. We can't stop everyone from coming in or traveling around once they're here, and if a terrorist is bent on suicide we can't stop him. Those are the realities of life in this brave new millennium.

More than three years have passed since the planes flew south from Boston and our world changed forever. There are nights when I wake up in a cold sweat and see it happening all over again, and on those nights I lie awake and wonder where we all went wrong and what the world is going to have to do to make amends.

Being a black man, my perspective on terrorism may be different from many Americans' perspective. A white woman who worked for the T at the time of the terrorist attacks said to me, "That was a terrible experience, Bob. I'm never going to feel safe in America again. Ever since that happened I've felt so uncertain about what's going to become of all of us." I said to her, "I've lived in America for fifty years and I've never felt safe." She gave me a strange look and said, "I don't understand." And I said, "What you experienced in New York is what I've experienced all of my life—looking over my shoulder, waiting for the other shoe to drop. I don't think as a white person you'll ever truly understand what that means—that no matter what you do, no matter how you do it, somebody's always watching you, waiting for you to slip up, for your blackness (other peoples negative expectations and beliefs) to show through." For African Americans, racism and its long term effects is a form of terrorism.

THE BOSTON SHOOTOUT

As I mentioned early on in this book, role models have been a big part of my life, starting with my parents, and then Yvonne Matthews and Jack Killgoar, who were enormous influences on my life at different stages of my development. When Ray introduced me to the Boston Shootout, I became involved in my way of becoming a role model for others, of giving something back. The Shootout was a premier basketball tournament established more than 25 years ago by Ken Hudson, the first black NBA referee, Yvonne Irving and Mrs. Wilson. The primary sponsors were Coca Cola, Northwest Airlines and John Hancock Insurance. Unfortunately, it no longer exists, but at the time, the Boston Shootout was a hot ticket for young athletes hoping for basketball hoop glory. Everything was donated to the tournament including airfare, hotel rooms, meals and vans. The kids who participated were treated like important people, many for the first time in their lives. They were taken to fine restaurants; they were given fancy new basketball sneakers; and not least of all they were offered the opportunity to play on the parquet floors of the famous Boston Garden. I made sure these kids knew how to act off the court too—that they dressed appropriately and comported themselves with dignity.

The Shootout has since been replaced by McDonalds' All American and Nike tournaments. But it began as a showcase for young high school athletes from all across the country to display their talents. I was a host of the Boston Shootout for 18 years. As a host I was responsible for my team from the time they stepped off the plane until I put them back on the plane for the flight home. Each Shootout consisted of eight teams from across the country (my team was New Orleans), and two coaches. Each team had a 16-passenger van, and the other seven hosts and I were responsible for everything from hospital runs to media events to practices to making sure the boys got in bed by curfew and stayed there till morning. When you're dealing with energetic young men whose hormones are in perpetual riot this is no easy feat. The hosts served as den fathers, and our principal mission was to show those youngsters that there was more to life than just basketball. Without hammering it at them, we let them know what we did professionally; we wanted to give them a sense of possibilities that lay beyond basketball and, without lecturing them, we tried to pass on some of our wisdom and experience. Those young men were focused on making it in the NBA. That was their dream. Without dampening their enthusiasm, we tried to sprinkle in a little realism, and without dwelling on the negative, we made it clear that the numbers were against them. Only two or three out of the hundred players who attended the Shootout each year made it to the NBA.

A few Shootout players, however, did go on to make their mark in the NBA, most notably Kerry Kittles, Juwan Howard, Grant Hill and Patrick Ewing. Over the lifetime of the Boston shootout 68 players were called up to the big time, but considering the thousands upon thousands who had that dream, the odds were stacked against those young men. It was my job to let them know that real people have real jobs that they take pride in. Their heroes didn't necessarily have to be the Michael Jordans and the Shaquille O'Neals of the world. Their heroes could be (and should be) their parents, their clergy, their teachers, their big brothers and sisters. I taught them that if basketball didn't pan out for them, they needed a solid foundation for life beyond sports. It was imperative to have a back up—and we drilled that into them. At that moment in their lives, their arena was basketball, but the chances were good that they would be forced to move on and make other choices. They needed to be prepared for that moment because a lot of bad things were out there waiting for them if they didn't—including dead-end jobs, drugs and crime. The Boston Shootout, in other words, was about more than basketball. It was sportsmanship and camaraderie and caring for one another and beginning to prepare for the rest of their lives.

In that short period of time, relationships were built and lessons learned outside the confines of the court. I got close to those youngsters; some of them loosened up enough to share their hopes and fears with me. I remember sitting in the van one day with rap music blaring and thinking that maybe I was too old for this. But then I smiled. I realized that being with those kids was keeping me young. And the payoff was priceless, because they knew that I genuinely cared for them and that I was taking time out of my life to be with them. We had interesting times together and it was probably one of the most enjoyable and relaxing times of my life. I felt enormous pride to be able to give back to the community by touching the lives of those young men. I had one-on-one conversations with those who would let themselves open up, and many of them felt that basketball was all they had, that it was their one chance to make a mark for themselves. It was their way out of poverty and without it they were less than zero. But I constantly fought against that negativity. I helped them see that there were other avenues, and I used my own story as an example of what could be done with less than world-class skills and talent. My mission was to provide them with realistic goals and a sense of hope. I tell the story of the Shootout because it is merely a continuation of the gift I received from my mentor and friends. The "Reach one Teach one" philosophy was a gift that kept on giving. To improve our future we all must reach back and lift up. In doing the Shootout for 18 years, I was honoring what I had so generously been given.

RETIREMENT

One night late in 2000 I had an epiphany. I just didn't want to play the game anymore. I had played long enough and I was bone tired, both in body and spirit. On that night of the epiphany I said to myself, "There's nothing else you can do here that's going to change anything." I had put in motion the things that I thought were important, things that were crying to be done, and there was nothing else for me as General Manager. The next GM, driven by his own fresh energy, would have his own promises to keep. As head of the T there is no guarantee that you will have forward momentum for more than, say, four or five years. Nobody lasts longer than that in the top job at the Authority, and if you try to stay longer, the crash and burn phase sets in. It was a major decision for me to say, "Okay, you're still riding the crest, but it's time to slip off the wave before it crashes." I had a very lucrative pension coming to me; I wouldn't have to work another day in my life if I didn't want to. I could sit around the house and do nothing, but that was not my plan. My goal was to write the book that you're holding in your hand.

Having made my decision, I sat down and wrote the following letter to Governor Jane Swift:

It is with mixed emotions that I tender my resignation as General Manager of the Massachusetts Bay Transportation Authority. It has been a great honor both personally and professionally to serve as General Manager of the MBTA. Growing up in Boston, my first memories of travel were with my mother along the old elevated portion of the Orange Line. As I look back with pride on our many accomplishments, I regret that I am leaving prior to joining you for the first ride on the Silver Line as we reintroduce service on Washington Street.

Under your direction, we initiated an era of service expansion and financial reform. Your strong policy guidance, along with support from Secretary Kevin J. Sullivan and the MBTA Board of Directors, have led to a level of excellence here at the MBTA that our passengers have come to expect. We have many things to be proud of including:

SERVICE

Over the last decade, ridership in the MBTA has risen by 20 percent, making the MBTA the only major urban transit system [in the US?] to experience such an increase. Our fares remain the lowest in the nation and we have significantly reduced the operating cost per mile. The MBTA has been recognized by APTA (American Public Transportation Association) for growing from the sixth largest to the fourth largest system in the United States.

Service expansions have broadened the T's reach. In 1997, the Old Colony railroad was completed and opened; in 1998, commuter rail service was extended to Newburyport; in 1999, Haverhill Station and Grafton Station were opened. Three stations will be opened between Worcester and Framingham in December of this year, and in 2001, the JFK Station was opened for commuter rail service.

In September 2000, construction of the Silver Line on Washington Street from Dudley Station to downtown Boston began. This line will serve as a replacement service for the Washington Street Corridor, which was served by the elevated portion of the Orange Line Subway until 1987. The project introduces state-of-the-art bus rapid transit and, once completed, is expected to serve 60,000 riders per day.

PLANNING

A Strategic Plan has seen developed and implemented for the first time in over 50 years. The Plan provides a clear description of the business and environment in which we operate, and will serve as a roadmap to guide the MBTA as it moves further into the new millennium. The Strategic Plan focuses on four areas—Service, Infrastructure, Finance, and People—and puts the emphasis on improved communication within the Authority as well as to its external constituencies.

The new planning process to steer the MBTA through financial reform (commonly referred to as forward funding) was implemented. Enhanced revenue streams, an annual public process for capital planning, and the best bond rating in the State, highlight the early accomplishments during the transition to "forward funding."

DIVERSITY

Minorities and women represent approximately 31.9 percent of the work-force at the T. Our commitment to the recruitment and promotion of women and minorities was recognized nationally by the Association of Public Transportation in 1998, when the MBTA was presented with its Minority and Women Advancement Award. A race neutral environment has been created, leveling the playing field in all aspects of the MBTA's business, including its contracts, and reflecting the diversity of the community it serves.

COMMUNITY COMMITMENTS

The "Customer Bill of Rights" was launched on February 21, 2001. As a result, the customer gained direct access to top personnel and received a complementary fare for delayed service. The T experienced a 3.5 percent increase in customer communications, took direct steps to improve service and rededicated itself to the mission of superior customer service.

In 1998, the MBTA Community Policing Patrol Plan was implemented to give the MBTA's passengers and neighbors a greater sense of security and comfort. The number of officers patrolling on trains and in stations has been increased from 18 to 92, and last year, the crime rate on the MBTA declined by 13.7 percent.

My tenure at the T was a joyful one. Twenty-five years ago, when I donned my first MBTA bus driver's uniform, I never dreamed I would have the opportunity to become the General Manager of the T. I am leaving the Authority with confidence that, under your strong leadership, the MBTA will continue to provide safe, accessible, dependable, clean and affordable transportation to our valued customers through the dedication of its diverse and talented workforce.

I thank you for the opportunity to serve your administration. I would look upon it as a privilege should you ever need me to serve you again. Please feel free to call on me if you may be in need of assistance.

Sincerely,

Robert Prince.

CODA

At the time I announced my retirement, the press interviewed a number of people about their reactions to my leaving, including a bus driver out of Quincy. The reporter asked him to describe me and he said, "Bob Prince is the same guy he was the day I met him driving a bus." He then told the reporter that he hadn't taken a day off in 23 years. He often felt sick and thought about staying home, but then he remembered the stories about me walking in that blizzard back in '76. He told himself that if Prince could get to the post-position every day, so could he. You never know how you affect anybody along the way. Being a black man in a white world, I always felt somewhat set apart, but stories like that lit a small fire inside of me. They warmed me. This man had not judged my color, but my actions.

I hadn't been with the Authority very long when I married Judith. Nobody from the T attended, except for a man named John. John had started working at the T a few years behind me, and I don't think that anybody knows I know John . John and I were fervent Bus rodeo enthusiasts, and we loved to attend the rodeos. The T holds two events to showcase operators' expertise—one is in bus, one is in rail. In 2001, Boston hosted the 9th Annual International Rail Rodeo. Rail jockeys from all over the United States and Canada converged on our city prepared to wheel T Orange Line cars for their respective cities. Operations on the Orange Line between Wellington Station and Oak Grove were suspended from 8 a.m. to noon as rail operators from New York to Los Angeles were tested on the rules of the rails, uniforms, equipment and customer service. Participants took Orange Line trains for a quick spin, and also took a written exam. These rail rodeos were held each year at different locations, sponsored by the American Public Transportation Association. The idea was to determine which transit agency had the best overall performance in the nation. It was wonderful fun!

One day, out of the blue, at a bus rodeo, John said something that stunned me. "I know it's hard to have a man tell you he's proud of you," he said. "But I'm very proud of you." I just looked at him, not sure how to react. "It's because you've never changed," he continued. "You're the same guy now that I knew when I came in. No different at all."

To me that was the highest of compliments.

I always worked hard not to let the power I had get caught up in my head. I wasn't about power. I saw myself as a representative of the MBTA with 6,500 voices. When I retired, I told the more than 700 people in attendance at my retirement celebration that I came to the job as an only child and I'm leaving with 6,500 brothers and sisters. I didn't use that observation as a piece of rhetoric; it was just the way I felt. And it's true that the T *is* like a family. You share a lot while you're working for the Authority. You share the birth of people's children, you share the death of loved ones, you share the trials and tribulations of the riding public. There is so much you carry with you that the general public will never truly understand. They may think the T is just another job, but if you do it right (and Lord knows, only time will tell you whether or not you did it right), it's not a job at all. It's a calling. It's your one chance to change people's lives for the better.

I worked to change people's lives for the better.

Those are the words I wouldn't mind having on my tombstone. I close this chapter on my journey with one of the many tributes I received at my retirement party. It seems that I was known as the MBTA's resident "poet," because I was always penning and delivered my "verse" at various functions. As I sat in the midst of family from across the country with friends and political officials, I was given the following tribute from one of my employees, Christine M. Bond, who probably knows more about me than most:

Robert Henry Prince Jr.
Twenty-five years is a very long time, to dedicate to an organization. We're happy to say that our General Manager is respected all over the transit nation. Robert Henry Prince Jr. is an impressive man with a history to support his stature. In twenty-five years he held twenty jobs from the bottom to the top. He faced every challenge of being the "first" and never did he stop.
Bob was a friend to his employees and a man who loves the T. With no hidden agenda, he is what you see. His ego is in check and I was always amazed that he didn't flaunt the power he had that so many people craved.
Twenty-Five years is a magnificent commitment for one person to make. The love that we felt from out General Manager was real; the man's not fake. He is a gentle man with a terrific human touch. He is known as "The People's General Manager", who is loved very much.
Bob told his employees he was proud of us, that we were number-one. He said when he took office there was much to be done. These statements were supported by what he was able to do because well being, caring and accomplishment soared during the years we were under you.
Twenty-Five years is quite an opportunity for one person to grow.

EVERYMAN

Robert Prince has graduated from the Harvard University of transit. His knowledge is valuable wherever he chooses to go.

As a Bus Operator during the Blizzard of 1978, Prince knew the T's culture is YOU SHOULD NEVER BE LATE. No buses were coming on that snowy day. Prince knew his Inspector did not play. So he started walking from his home on the hill. He overlooked the snow, he overlooked the chill. No vehicles were coming he could not take a seat. The man relied on strong will and two very frozen feet. More that fifteen miles later, yes he walked to Quincy's bus garage, the legend of Prince began that day he made his Inspector proud.

Twenty-five years in one organization, the stories Bob Prince must hold! From Bus Operator to General Manager in a quarter of a century, the year the T turned 100 years old.

Legend has it that the original subway rider was a black cat—a feline—who took a ride on the first subway line. They say the cat showed up one day and would not go away so they named that black cat " The Prince of the Subway.. That was 1897 and 100 years later another Prince was named the King. Bobby, little did your mother know when she was taking you on the T, that her only son would be the first African General Manager, a part of the T's proud history. Even though Mom can't be here, Dad is and his heart sings!

Twenty-five years of such dedication is impressive your record shows. We love you we're proud of you; we hate to see you go. You helped a lot of people and you did it quietly. Thanks for all that you've given to your MBTA family.

This poem summed up my experience and it's hard to read. I am humbled by the sentiment. It's quite a tribute for a person seen as "just average," a person not remembered by his elementary school Principal ......a regular "Joe Average"

7587220R0

Made in the USA
Charleston, SC
20 March 2011